DATE DUE			

Transatlantic
Trends in
Retailing

Recent Titles from QUORUM BOOKS

Microeconomic Concepts for Attorneys: A Reference Guide
Wayne C. Curtis

Beyond Dumping: New Strategies for Controlling Toxic Contamination
Bruce Piasecki, Editor

Payments in the Financial Services Industry of the 1980s: Conference Proceedings
Federal Reserve Bank of Atlanta, Sponsor

Japanese Business Law and the Legal System
Elliott J. Hahn

YOUTHJOBS: Toward a Private/Public Partnership
David Bresnick

State Government Export Promotion: An Exporter's Guide
Alan R. Posner

Principles for Electric Power Policy
Technology Futures, Inc., and Scientific Foresight, Inc.

The Debt Dilemma of Developing Nations: Issues and Cases
Chris C. Carvounis

Business and Technological Dynamics in Newly Industrializing Asia
Wenlee Ting

Employee Development Programs: An Organizational Approach
Bobby C. Vaught, Frank Hoy, and W. Wray Buchanan

International Accounting: Issues and Solutions
Ahmed Belkaoui

Witness Intimidation: The Law's Response
Michael H. Graham

Transatlantic Trends in Retailing

Takeovers and Flow of Know-How

Madhav P. Kacker

Q

Quorum Books

Westport, Connecticut • London, England

Library of Congress Cataloging in Publication Data

Kacker, M. P.
 Transatlantic trends in retailing.

 Bibliography: p.
 Includes index.
 1. Retail trade—United States—Foreign ownership.
2. Investments, Foreign—United States. 3. Franchises
(Retail trade) 4. Investments, American. I. Title.
HF5429.3.K34 1985   381 '.1 '0973   84-15928
ISBN 0-89930-036-7 (lib. bdg.)

Library of Congress Catalog Card Number: 84-15928
ISBN: 0-89930-036-7

First published in 1985 by Quorum Books

Greenwood Press
A division of Congressional Information Service, Inc.
88 Post Road West
Westport, Connecticut 06881

Printed in the United States of America

10 9 8 7 6 5 4 3 2 1

Copyright Acknowledgments

Grateful acknowledgment is given for permission to use the following:

Data gathered during field study in Europe and the United States for an earlier study made in
1982 funded by the Conference Board, used with permission from the Conference Board, New
York.

Appendix to Chapter 4 "Our Belgian Friends" reproduced from *The Profile*, December 1982,
permission given by Food Town Stores, Salisbury, N.C.

Figure 5.1 from *Retail Planning in the European Community*, edited by Ross L. Davies,
permission to reprint given by Gower Publishing Company Ltd., Farnborough, England.

Figure 6.1 from 'The Bulletin', Spring 1982, permission to reprint given by Bi-Lo Stores, Mauldin, S.C.

Table 8.2 from Donald W. Hackett, "The International Expansion of U.S. Franchise Systems: Status and Strategies," *Journal of International Business Studies*, Vol. 7 (Spring 1976), p. 68, reprinted with permission from the editor.

Table 8.3 from Bruce J. Walker and Michael J. Etzel, "The Internationalization of U.S. Franchise Systems: Progress and Procedure," *Journal of Marketing*, vol. 37 (April 1973), p. 45, reprinted with permission from the American Marketing Association.

Appendix A, "Some Comments on International Retailing," reprinted with permission from Dr. Stanley C. Hollander, East Lansing, Mich.

Appendix B, "Multinational Retailing: Are the Food Chains Different," *Comité International des Entreprises à Succursales*, no. 8, Paris, 1973, reprinted with permission from Dr. James B. Jefferys.

Appendix C, Speech delivered by Dr. A.C.R. Dreesmann at the Annual Convention of the National Retail Merchants Association, held in Tokyo in 1980, reprinted with permission from National Retail Merchants Association, New York.

Contents

Figures

Tables

Introduction

The complexion of international retailing has changed dramatically in the past few years, evidenced by a phenomenal exchange of retailing ideas and techniques among countries. Many companies, both retailing and non-retailing, are expanding into international markets by establishing or acquiring retail business firms. Sears took its self-service and department store concepts to Cuba and then to many other Latin American countries. Sears' international commitment took on new dimension in 1982 when it started an autonomous international trading company. Sears and several others such as Safeway, Southland, and McDonald's are presenting new retailing concepts and management techniques throughout the world.

The internationalization of retailing has also taken the route of acquisitions, a trend that became conspicuous in the 1970s when a number of European companies invested in the U.S. retailing industry. Since 1975, over $2 billion worth of foreign investments, mostly from West European countries, have poured into U.S. retailing and the hotel-restaurant industry. There have been a series of noteworthy acquisitions: Grand Union, by Cavenham (British); Gimbels and Saks Fifth Avenue, by Brown & Williamson (British); Fed mart, by Mann GmbH (German); Dillard and Outlet Stores, by Vroom & Dreesmann (Dutch); A&P Stores, by the Tengelmann Group (German); and Korvettes, by Agache Willot (French). The year 1979 was especially critical in the annals of American retailing. The year not only witnessed four leading U.S. retail chains of this country passing into European hands but also recorded an infructuous takeover encounter between Brascan Ltd., a Canadian holding company, and F. W. Woolworth Company, which was celebrating its centenary. The pace of acquisitions has continued in the 1980s, though it has somewhat slowed.

Changes in ownership and control have not been always followed by an improvement in the financial performance of the acquired companies. In fact, two well-established retail chains, Korvettes in the East and Fed Mart in the West, went into liquidation within a few years of their acquisition by European companies. In many cases, the foreign investors have been criticized for their inept decision. They seemed to ignore the point that owning a retail store is one thing but running it in a diverse socio-cultural setting is quite a different game. The challenge was not just confined to managing a real estate. It rather lay in dealing with an intricate subsystem, comprising suppliers, financiers, employees, manufacturers, and consumers, without which no retail operation can survive in the United States.

This book assesses prevailing trends in international retailing. It particularly examines the trend of European investments in the U.S. retail industry. The focus is on the transatlantic region, the area where a significant part of total investment in retailing has flowed during the last two decades. In addition to providing data on the flow of investments and profiles of major investors, the book addresses the following questions:

What structural changes have taken place in European retailing in recent years?

What might be the primary motivation for a foreign company to make direct investments in the U.S. retail industry?

What happens to the acquired companies after foreign capital is pumped in with respect to organizational changes, strategy formulation, action programs, and exchange of retailing know-how?

What has been the role of U.S. companies in overseas retailing, particularly in franchising?

The book first examines the European economic and political environment in order to provide readers with the background for understanding the trend in international retailing. Chapter 2 looks at the retailing scene in Europe in the context of the overall economic environment. It describes briefly some of the emerging trends that have characterized European retailing. Chapter 3 portrays various dimensions of the trend, providing statistical data from the U.S. Department of Commerce. Chapter 4 presents a profile of major investors showing that most participants in the game were not new to international retailing.

Chapters 5 and 6 look at the motivations of foreign investors and examine the microlevel and macrolevel factors that have impelled foreigners to invest sizable sums in retailing. Chapter 6 focuses on the strategic and operational changes introduced and implemented in the acquired U.S. retail companies. To provide a balanced view of the situation, the extent of involvement of U.S. companies in overseas retailing, particularly in promoting retail franchising, is presented in chapters 7 and 8. The current status of the U.S. retail industry and the mergers and acquisitions among the domestic retail companies is the subject of chapter 9. Finally, chapter 10 sums up the discussion and makes concluding observations. The main text is supported in the end by three appendixes containing texts of articles or speeches by three leading experts in the field of international retailing: Stanley Hollander, James Jefferys and Anton Dreesmann. The comments and observations of these authors have added some new dimensions to the primary focus of this book.

A project such as this could not have been undertaken without the support and cooperation of several organizations and individuals. First, my gratitude goes to the Conference Board for its grant and for bringing me in contact with many companies in the United States and Europe. In particular, I thank James Greene, who not only provided much-needed administrative support but was a source of some innovative ideas, which enriched this study. I am grateful to the Conference Board for permission to use the data collected in the original study they sponsored in 1982.

I am indebted to many executives and their respective organizations who welcomed my visit and provided some valuable insights on the foreign acquisitions trend. Special mention may be made of Guy Beckers, president, Delhaize de Lion; Michel DeRoy, president, Docks de France; Albert Heijn, president, Ahold N.V.; A.C.R. Dreesmann, chairman and chief executive officer, Vendex International; R. P. Van der Kind from Koninklijke Bijenkorf Beheer (KBB), J. F. Riviere from Promodes; and the Hugo Mann Group in Germany. Several executives from the acquired companies in the United States were of great help: Lawson Saul, president, Bi-Lo; William Stewart, president, Red Food Stores; and Ralph Ketner, chairman, Food Town Stores. I thank all of them.

I also thank James Jefferys, general secretary, International Association of Department Stores; Stanley Hollander, Michigan State University; David Rachman, City University of New York, Baruch College; and Barry Berman, Hofstra University, for stimulating discussions on this subject at various meetings.

Here at Suffolk University, I would not have met the deadlines and finished this project without the encouragement of Richard McDowell, dean of the School of Management, and David Wheeler, chairperson of marketing department. My gratitude goes to them. I thank my colleague Nizamettin Aydin for useful suggestions and Robert Peacock who undertook an excellent data search in several libraries. Special mention must be made of the help provided by the Faculty Resource Unit in having the manuscript typed and reproduced in time. Thanks go to Sara Leefman, Annmarie Bertino, and Carol Matz for accepting at times a tight schedule. At Greenwood Press, I am very thankful to Lynn Taylor and her editorial staff for their interest and continued cooperation throughout this project.

Finally, I express a deep indebtedness to my wife, Vijai, for her patience, time, and moral support throughout the duration of this project.

Transatlantic
Trends in
Retailing

1

Economic and Political Trends in Europe

Many significant economic and political trends have emerged in the European environment during the last 25 years, both integrative and disintegrative in character. In 1958, six European nations—France, Germany, Italy, Netherlands, Belgium, and Luxembourg—joined together to form the world's biggest economic and political union, the European Common Market. Following an earlier model of the Benelux countries, this group took a historic move toward creating a customs union and an administrative structure designed to safeguard economic stability and set prices for critical agricultural and nonagricultural produce.

The creation of the European Common Market exercised a tremendous influence on other free market economies in Europe, including Denmark, the United Kingdom, Ireland, and Greece, which began to appreciate the need for economic unity and decided to join the group. Austria, Norway, Portugal, Sweden, Switzerland, and Iceland formed the European Free Trade Association (EFTA), eliminating internal tariffs but with no common external tariff like the Common Market had. Spain and Portugal are still trying to gain entry to the Common Market.

Soon after the formation of the Common Market, many multinationals (MNCs), especially from the United States and Japan, began making significant direct investments by setting up plants in the European Economic Community (EEC) countries. By the late sixties, European markets were flooded with U.S. products. One estimate was that nearly half of the goods advertised on British television were made by U.S. companies. Most investments made by U.S. MNCs were in nontraditional and technology-intensive fields, such as computers, synthetic rubber, and photographics.[1]

Europeans' long-cherished dreams of economic union were dashed by economic pressures that originated from the 1973 oil crisis, which triggered a series of economic ills: cost-push inflation at unprecedented levels and a high rate of unemployment that severely affected the economies of member nations. This development led most countries to look to their individual interests and maintain self-integrity rather than group integrity. Thus, the 1970s witnessed some disintegrative trends even though the beginning of this decade was heralded by the entry of the U.K. in the ECM group.

COOPERATION IN THE PRIVATE SECTOR

Mounting competition from Japan and the United States has led some leading European MNCs to consider making concerted efforts in the sphere of research and development and advanced technology. In April 1983, for example, seventeen heads of corporations met in Paris to deliberate on this issue.[2] In spite of apparent failures to build a common ground and develop compatible standards, some progress seems to have come in the form of agreements among leading MNCs—for example, the Philips and CGE agreement on telephone exchanges, the Philips-Thorn EMI agreement on videodiscs, and Philips' expected agreement with four German cable makers for manufacturing fiber optics.

The second noteworthy event that has taken place recently is the establishment of the European Strategic Program for Research in Information Technology (ESPRIT), designed to promote cooperation in the critical sector of information technology. It is believed that the EEC will provide financial support to this program to the extent of 50 percent, and three leading corporations—ICL, Siemens, and CII-Honeywell-Bull—will collaborate on a joint laboratory.

Third, the member nations of the European Postal and Telecommunications Commission, some of them outside Western Europe, have recently agreed on steps to harmonize their telecommunications technology and establish common technical standards, mainly to help the telecommunications industry defend itself against growing U.S. competition.[3] Such joint moves indicate that despite occasional rifts and differences, the European countries are forging an economic and technological unity.

On the darker side, several attempts by MNCs to pool resources and enter into joint ventures to meet foreign competition have failed. The Thomson-Grundig venture was going to be the first serious effort to meet Japanese competition in the field of consumer electronics, but the project never took off. Furthermore, the manufacturers could not agree on a single color television standard, which explains the present coexistence of two incompatible systems, PAL and SECAM. PAL stands for Phase Alternation Line, characteristic of West German color television system. SECAM stands for Sequence de Couleurs avec Memoire which is the French color television system. The two companies located on the Rhine, across from each other, had merger plans to create a united front in consumer electronics against Japan. The initial talks between the two were quite encouraging but a conclusive stage could never be reached. The nationalistic considerations came in the way. Nor was there any success in formulating a joint standard on satellite communication when the British backed away and decided to adopt U.S. standards on a radio-telephone system.

One important reason for the frequent collapse of integrative efforts is the pressure on many companies to achieve higher rates of economic growth by moving outside the Continent, growth that in many cases was thwarted by an unprecedented rise in price levels. The result was that most governments were forced to back out of integrated programs to improve their own balance of payments instead, adopting protectionist measures and imposing sanctions to support the growth of indigenous industries and meet political promises.

In the past, most European companies moved to neighboring countries; now many are going outside the Continent to exploit market opportunities. According to a Conference Board study, when asked where they anticipated significant growth in the next ten years, 90 percent of responding European companies thought that the major growth would occur in at least one continent outside Europe, 60 percent expected expansion in at least two continents other than Europe, and 40 percent thought that they would cover three continents other than Europe.[4]

The promise of the EEC has been only partly fulfilled. It is often complained that the Common Market is no longer as common as it used to be; there is a lot of red tape at national boarders. The paperwork and the time involved at the community's internal frontiers at the time of crossing borders means substantial additional cost to exporters, estimated in some cases at between 5 and 10 percent of the final selling price of certain products. Truck drivers may spend several hours getting clearance from appropriate authorities.[5]

The primary organs of the EEC—the Commission of the European Communities, the Council of Ministers, and the European Parliament—operate in an atmosphere of tension. The intensity and degree of such conflicts hinge to a great extent on the compatibility of interests of individual members. Because decisions are dependent on unanimity among ministers, the issues often need to be referred to national governments for comment and approval, a process that can become time-consuming. It is believed that with the development of deeper unanimity of interests, member nations eventually will favor a majority voting system to expedite decision making.

A significant event in the history of European economic integration was direct election to the European Parliament held for the first time in June 1979; however, the parliament still does not enjoy that power which would enable it to deal effectively with the Council of Ministers and the commission.

The gradual abolition of tariffs between EFTA and the EEC since 1960 has brought about the world's largest free trade area; there are 17 European nations with a combined market of 310 million people. The commercial bond among these countries is expected to intensify as external challenges increase. The community is now moving toward setting up a common monetary system, such as a central bank and fixed exchange rates. No doubt progress will be slow because all steps toward a uniform monetary and fiscal policy will pose threats to the national sovereignty of member countries. As has been borne out by recent meetings of the European Commission, there exists little unanimity among EEC members. Many times deliberations in these meetings are marked by unpleasant dissension. Therefore the pace of further integration is likely to be slow until a stage is reached when the economies of member countries become strong enough to withstand the pains of short-run sacrifices essential for consummating common goals. According to a Business International Survey, most international companies operating in Europe believed that the EEC will manage to preserve its imperfect customs union but may not progress much further toward a truly unified market.[6]

A Business International Survey of executive opinion showed that most European countries are likely to have a slower rate of economic growth during the 1980s compared to the 1960s and 1970s, when they experienced unusually high expansion. A majority of executives identified slower economic growth as one of the factors that would have the greatest impact on their operations in Europe during the 1980s. Other such factors identified in this survey were increasing competition within Western Europe, the cost of labor and energy, the effect of inflation and unstable currencies, unemployment and resulting job protection, and sociopolitical uncertainties. The anticipated slow growth they attributed to the end of the postwar boom, stagnating population, saturation of markets, structural overcapacities in industries like steel, textiles, and chemicals, diminishing productivity gains, large surpluses built by OPEC countries (especially Saudi Arabia and the Gulf States), and the inflationary pressures that have tended to inhibit growth at least in the industrialized countries of Europe. It was widely held that the growth rates will tend to be higher in southern Europe than in the north.[7]

RELATIONS WITH SOVIET BLOC NATIONS

As far as relations between Western Europe and the Soviet bloc are concerned, political factors probably will continue to be more important than economic factors, although it is likely that economic interdependence between the two blocs will grow, despite political interference from within and outside. Soviet imports from Common Market countries are estimated to be around $13.2 billion a year, as shown in figure 1.1. Although a ban was imposed by the EEC on Soviet imports in 1981 to protest the declaration of martial law in Poland, the ban affected only 1.4 percent of Soviet exports to member countries. Some member countries welcomed the ban more because it amounted to trade protectionism rather than anti-Soviet feeling. Recently the Common Market Commission decided to drop this economic sanction, despite opposition from some European enterprises.[8]

The growing prospects of energy supply from the Soviet Union have led to one of the most unpredictable economic collaborations in East-West trade: the construction of a 5,500-kilometer pipeline from the gasfields of western Siberia to Western Europe for annual deliveries of 40 billion cubic meters of natural gas to Austria, Belgium, France, the Federal Republic of Germany, Italy, the Netherlands, and Switzerland. Despite some belief that the Soviet Union, as a single negotiator, took undue advantage of the deal with a competing group of West European bidders, many believe that the pipeline contracts have proved to be of mutual benefit and will accelerate the progress of East-West trade linkages. Most pipeline equipment was bought by the Soviet Union in Western Europe, providing significant support to ailing steel industries in Italy and France. Moreover, the Soviet Union is believed to be a much more reliable trading partner than OPEC countries. For example, it has never threatened customers with an interruption of energy supply for political reasons, as the United States did regarding the supply of enriched uranium to West Germany.[9]

Figure 1.1
Soviet Trade, 1982 (billions of dollars)

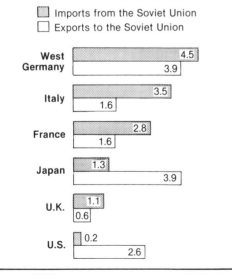

Source: OECD   *Estimates

West Germany has been the largest trading partner of the Soviet Union; the relationship began in 1855 when Siemans laid a telegraph line in czarist Russia. Exports from West Germany to the Soviet Union accounted for 2.2 percent of its total exports in 1982, estimated at $3.9 billion. For Mannesmann A.G., a steel manufacturer and a major exporter of gas pipelines, the shipment of pipeline equipment to the Soviet Union accounted for 18 percent of its worldwide exports and 8 percent of its total sales in 1982.

Serious political differences have not interfered with German-Russian trade. Ulrich Steger, a leading spokesman of Germany's Social Democratic party, described the situation well when he observed, "There are some people who think East-West trade is immoral. We like to separate trade and politics. If you once start and say, I don't trade with the Soviet Union because it is a military dictatorship, then I wonder how many countries we could actually trade with."[10] The trade relationship between the Soviet Union and France is also improving. The two countries signed an economic cooperation agreement in February 1984 to increase trade between them. France has signed contracts to buy more Soviet natural gas valued at $1.6 billion and has indicated that it would sell a technologically advanced telephone exchange system to the Soviets, despite U.S. protests.

POLITICAL COMPLEXION OF WESTERN EUROPE

Social Democrats currently form the largest group in the European Parliament and thus are the most important political entity in Western Europe. In almost every West European country, the Socialists or Social Democrats either have been in power or have worked as the main opposition party. Socialists are now in power in Italy, Portugal, France, and Spain; they are the main opposition party in the Netherlands, the United Kingdom, and West Germany. Italy claims to have Western Europe's largest Communist party. Another notable feature of the current political scene is that while northern and central Europe continue to swing to the right, southern Europe seems to be tilting to the left. The results of April 1983 elections in Iceland, Austria, and Portugal have substantiated this trend. The Socialists lost in Iceland and Austria but not in Portugal. No party, however, was able to gain an overall majority, which means that political trends in Europe will continue to remain volatile.

In the course of a Business International Survey of executives from international companies operating in Europe, the respondents showed little concern for the strong socialistic trends dominating the political climate in most European countries. A U.K. firm dismissed the question of Communist participation in governments, whereas a German executive said, "Personally, I believe that at least in the short run, Communist participation in the government in Italy would have positive results—but in the long term, things might look otherwise."[11] A number of executives, however, expressed concern about the prevalence of weak and unstable governments in Europe.

Despite the emergence of socialistic forces in France and Italy and the installation of a conservative government in Great Britain during the past decade, the governments of these countries are moving with caution and keeping economic priorities in the forefront, without getting bogged down with political ideologies. The socialistic governments in France and Italy are more worried now about maintaining the growth of a medium-sized enterprise sector and have slowed the trend of government takeovers. Even the Labour government in Britain before the last election was not too enthusiastic about state takeovers or continuing to pay subsidies indefinitely to loss-making state enterprises. The new Conservative government has also adopted a moderate stand. It has only trimmed, not abolished, programs of public support for sectors such as microelectronics and the declining sectors such as ship building.[12]

In 1968, J. J. Servan-Schreiber prophesied that the world's third greatest industrial power, just after the United States and the Soviet Union, would be not Europe but American industry in Europe, unless the Europeans woke up and met the challenge. Servan-Schreiber was overwhelmed by the dominant sprawling of U.S. MNCs over the Continent and was unable to foresee the economic forces that emerged in the 1970s and significantly affected the existing balance of economic power. The supremacy of U.S. MNCs has been challenged by Japanese, German, French, and even Third World countries like Brazil, Mexico, and South Korea for the following reasons. First, European and Japanese companies, which had traditionally lagged in engineering, manufacturing, marketing, and financial expertise, rapidly caught up with U.S. companies. The Europeans became fairly competitive and developed analytical and planning skills characteristic of U.S. management. Second, the period of the 1960s was noted for a significant amount of postwar reconstruction, corporate mergers, and consolidations in Western Europe and Japan. The average size of companies expanded in this region, adding to their capability to exploit new economies of scale in production, marketing, and R&D. Many made extraordinary profits during this period, enabling them to strengthen their financial and R&D base and improve their managerial know-how.[13]

Third, the extent of public ownership of business enterprises increased significantly in many West European countries. Nationalized enterprises are involved in the production of goods and services that range from cars and trucks to pots and pans and operating hotels and airlines. The share of the public sector in total national investment varies from 20 percent in West Germany, to 25 percent in Britain, 55 percent in France, and 65 percent in Austria. Retailing is a predominantly private enterprise activity in most countries. Governmental involvement in commercial activity makes it obligatory for it to make vital decisions in matters such as pricing, purchasing, plant location, diversification, product development, and labor relations. It is believed that public ownership enables the government to implement effectively its economic and industrial policies promoting employment, regional development, and social emancipation. It is possible to revitalize ailing units through financial grants and subsidies, which no government would venture to do in the event of private ownership.

LEGAL ENVIRONMENT OF BUSINESS

Most European countries have introduced significant new laws during the past two decades regarding the newly emerging business institutions, following the establishment of the European Community. The new laws seek to restrict and regulate the growth of big business to ensure that small businesses survive and economic power is not monopolized by one or more companies in a given industry. Soon after its creation, the EEC initiated the process of developing a legal framework to regulate business activity, with the overriding objective of facilitating economic integration. Thus, it took steps to ensure that business firms do not create obstacles to the free flow of goods and services through contractual prohibitions related to prices, territories, and other matters. Articles 85 and 86 of the Treaty of Rome clearly stipulate the desire of the EEC to preserve free and fair competition, patterned after sections 1 and 2 of the Sherman Anti-Trust Act. The member countries have also taken steps to strengthen their antitrust laws. According to some experts, West Germany has the toughest and most comprehensive antitrust laws outside the United States. Recently Great Britain passed a stiff competition bill that identified seven areas of competition to be investigated, ranging from supply restrictions of retailers to discriminatory pricing.[14]

With the emergence of large shopping centers and hypermarkets in many West European countries, the authorities in these countries took legislative actions in the direction of land use control, environmental protection, and protection of small retailers. These regulatory measures will be discussed later in this book.

NOTES

1. "Star-Spangled Menace," *Marketing Magazine*, February 1, 1969, p. 31.

2. "Europe Moves to Harmonize Communication," *Wall Street Journal*, January 23, 1984, p. 27.

3. "European Industry and Multinationals: New Spirit of Cooperation," *Multinational Info.*, no. 2 (Institute for Research and Information on Multinationals May 1983), p. 6.

4. Ronald Berenbeium, *Managing the International Company: Building a Global Perspective* (New York: The Conference Board, 1982).

5. "European Community—The Impurities Are Not Just in the Beer," *Economist*, October 22, 1983, p. 49.

6. Peter W. Wood and Robert F. Elliot, "Trading Blocs and Common Markets," in Ingo Walter and Tracy Murray, eds., *Handbook of International Business* (New York: John Wiley, 1982), pp. 4-42; "Europe in the 1980s, Corporate Forecasts and Strategies," *Business International S.A.* (February 1979): 103.

7. "Europe in the 1980's," pp. 13-20.

8. "Common Market Nations Decide to Drop Trade Sanctions against Soviet Union," *Wall Street Journal*, December 23, 1983, p. 12.

9. For a critical analysis, see Gordon Crovitz, "Europe Pays for Its Pipe Dream," *Wall Street Journal*, December 13, 1983, p. 30; Letter to the Editor from Dietmar K. Winje, "Europeans Still High on Soviet Gas," *Wall Street Journal*, December 28, 1983, p. 13.

10. Roger Thurow, "German Firms Cultivate Soviet Trade," *Wall Street Journal*, November 16, 1983, p. 34.

11. "Europe in the 1980's," p. 105.

12. Lawrence Franko, "European Industrial Policy: Past, Present and Future" (Conference Board in Europe, Brussels: February 1980), p. 51.

13. Earl H. Fry, *Financial Invasion of the U.S.A.* (New York: McGraw-Hill, 1980), p. 35.

14. Philips R. Cateora, *International Marketing* (Homewood, Ill: Richard D. Irwin, 1983), p. 212.

2

European Retailing at a Crossroad

The retailing industry in Europe stands at a crossroad today. The industry is dominated by independent small or medium-sized downtown stores with a narrow product focus. Although this sector is gradually declining in terms of the number of business units and their share of total retail turnover, it still commands a good deal of market power and has proved to be a formidable hurdle in the modernization and upscaling of retailing institutions in many countries. The independent small retailers have built strong lobbies to influence government decisions and are represented on decision-making bodies responsible for approving additions to or expansion of existing retail facilities.

Despite their power and respect, the institution of the independent downtown retailer has not been able to do much to prevent the entry of large-scale retailers and the adoption of retailing innovations from other countries. Among the strong environmental forces that facilitated the inflow of new retailing techniques and institutions in Europe was the increasing urbanization that began in the early fifties and led to downtown congestion and the development of residential areas on the outskirts of towns and cities. This heralded a new era in Europe, as it did in the United States, marked by changes in living styles and buying habits. It helped the emergence and development of neighborhood and regional shopping centers, with new concepts of self-service, somewhat scrambled (diversified) merchandising, and even discount retailing. The 1973 oil crisis led to severe recession and high rates of inflation and unemployment, severely affecting the economic growth of most European countries. The oil crisis created internal pressure in many retailing companies to reduce distribution costs and look for greater efficiency. Many traditional small retailers could not survive these pressures. Some closed; others sought new locations, expanded the merchandise mix, and adopted new techniques such as self-service and other methods to enhance operational efficiency, such as the pooling of resources by creating voluntary chains of cooperatives. Still, a great many preferred to adhere to their traditional operations and successfully influenced public policy to create legal barriers against the entry of large-scale and more innovative retail institutions.

The two decades 1960 to 1980 were a period of turbulence and witnessed significant changes in European retailing. Two diametrically opposite events occurred: fierce survival battles fought by small retailers on one side and the emergence of gigantic hypermarkets on the other. This chapter focuses on major structural changes in European retailing that began in the mid-1950s and have continued. It also highlights the leadership role played by some European companies in the development of new retailing techniques and institutions such as no-frill box stores, price-clubs and hypermarkets.

STRUCTURAL CHANGES IN EUROPEAN RETAILING

Several structural changes have occurred in European retailing since the early 1960s. These changes indicate that the retailing industry in Europe has responded to environmental pressures by adopting new techniques and introducing innovative changes in traditional practices and operations.

Since 1960, there has been a gradual decline in the role of middleman in the purchasing and distribution of consumer products, particularly food lines. Synchronized with this one sees a dramatic rise in self-service. Self-service was introduced in the United States in 1938. Sweden and Germany took an early lead in adopting this practice and taking other important steps to streamline the distribution system. In Germany, the proportion of retail food stores with a turnover below DM 250,000 fell from 98.6 percent to 80.8 percent between 1958 and 1969. In these stores, turnover as a percentage of total retail sales in food line dropped from 76.8 percent to 32.2 percent during this period. The share of self-service in total German food retail sales jumped from 34.8 percent in 1960 to 87.1 percent in 1969, about the same level as in Sweden. A similar pattern, though somewhat slower, was seen in food retailing in the United Kingdom and the Netherlands.[1]

The total number of retail establishments has been stagnant or gradually declining in many European countries. This is happening along with a slow rate of population growth. As table 2.1 shows, the rate of population growth during 1970-1980 has been 0.5 percent or less in twelve of seventeen countries, with West Germany and Switzerland accounting for a zero rate of growth. The fall in birthrates was noted in all European countries with the exception of Ireland and Greece, and a slowdown of net immigration in recent years has resulted in a shrinkage of the potential retail market for consumer goods, exercising additional pressure on inefficient small retailers to withdraw.

West Germany introduced the discount store concept in Europe in the early 1950s. The number of discount houses in West Germany increased from 27 in 1957 to over 300 in 1963 and well over 1,000 in 1970. By 1980, the number had reached around 2,000 stores, with much bigger average size and volume. The concept of discount retailing slowly spread to other countries in Europe; however, the emphasis was confined to food and soft goods lines as opposed to the United States, where discounting embraced hard lines.

The number of supermarkets and variety chain stores grew significantly during this period, along with postwar reconstruction programs. In France, the sales accounted for by large-scale retailers almost doubled between 1950 and 1965. The number of variety chain stores increased from 150 to over 600 and that of independent grocers declined by 20 percent during the same period.[2]

Table 2.1

Demographic Trends and Growth of Retailing Facilities in Selected West European Countries

Country	Population, 1980-1981 (thousand)	Population Growth Rate, 1970-1980	GNP per Capita	Number of Units in Retail Trade		
				1978	1979	1980
Austria	7,554	0.1	9,360	32,842	38,661	37,148
Belgium	9,861	.2	11,120	129,889	130,113	129,627
Denmark	5,122	.4	12,010	n.a.	n.a.	n.a.
Finland	4,801	.4	9,700	35,493		
France	53,963	.5	11,200	—	411,000	413,000
West Germany	61,666	.0	12,320	344,752		
Italy	56,223	.5	6,400	927,372[a]		
Luxembourg	364	.5	15,100	3,956	3,878	
Netherlands	14,246	.8	11,010	n.a.	n.a.	n.a.
Norway	4,100	.5	12,830	33,132[b]	32,928[c]	32,860[d]
Portugal	9,826	1.2	2,300	13,597[b]	15,240[c]	15,837[d]
Sweden	8,324	.3	13,730	49,866	51,096	54,506
Switzerland	6,473	.0	15,980	n.a.	n.a.	n.a.
United Kingdom	56,005	.1	8,520	234,785	235,174	228,409

SOURCE: (a) 1981 Statistical Yearbook (New York, United Nations, 1983)
(b) Statistical Yearbook 1979/1980 (New York, United Nations, 1981)
(c) World Bank Atlas (Washington D.C., International Bank for Reconstruction and Development, 1983)

[a]1971 data.
[b]1977 data.
[c]1978 data.
[d]1979 data.

In Stockholm, an innovative style of food retailing originated in the early 1960s with the setting up of Hemkop (home shop), which sold food products and a limited range of nonfood items at a discount, using a catalog, telephone orders, and home delivery service.[3] This retailing type found its niche in market segments consisting of families without cars, which needed both home delivery as well as low prices.

With the growth of supermarkets and large variety chains, competition intensified between traditional retail trade and the new stores. One way the independent retailers responded to this competition was by organizing themselves into voluntary chains. The emergence of voluntary chains of single-line retail stores revolutionized the retail distribution in nonfood trades, especially in the Nordic region. Scandinavian countries rank above the average European country in sales and number of persons engaged per retail establishment. These countries rank quite high in the matter of self-service in food trade and are also a stronghold of consumer cooperatives.[4] Swedish merchants also formed themseleves into buying groups and joined together as a sort of collective of department stores in a competitive move. These collective department stores had the advantage of certain common facilities such as administrative offices and restaurants.[5]

Thus, throughout Europe, the number of critical buying points in retail trade fell down, especially in food retailing. Retailers concentrated into bigger organizations and thus acquired greater bargaining power. In Sweden, three distribution organizations control approximately 80 percent of the total retail market for food items. The concentration has spread internationally with multinational buying organizations like Nordisk Handelsforbund, which acts as a joint buying agent for the cooperative wholesale societies of five Nordic countries. In Switzerland, cooperatives account for one-fifth of all retail establishments and about 25 percent of total retail sales. Two giant Swiss cooperative organizations share one-third of the total retail business, leaving two-thirds in the hands of independent small stores.[6] In Germany, too, supermarket chains are resorting to joint purchasing to get more favorable terms from the manufacturers.

This combination-cooperative movement has strengthened significantly the position of retail buyers, with more suppliers chasing a smaller number of organized buyers. It has also enabled many retail organizations to implement their own marketing programs and sell a part of retail merchandise under private labels.

SOME RECENT TRENDS

In recent years, the share of retailers' private brand products in total grocery sales in Britain has shown a significant rise from an average of 22 or 23 percent to 25 percent. British supermarket chains have been squeezing their margins and replacing an increasing number of manufacturers' brands with goods sold under their own labels. This trend, likely to intensify in the near future, may affect retail trade in other European countries; it has already hurt the business of many national food manufacturers such as Procter & Gamble, Heinz, Cadbury, Watney's, Kellogg's, and Birdseye.[7] The chains of Sainsbury and Tesco are especially noted for selling grocery items under private labels.

There has been a significant rise in concentration of grocery retailing. At the beginning of the 1970s, four leading retailing groups in Great Britain had the following market share: Allied Group, 7.9 percent; Tesco, 7.2 percent; Fine Fare, 4.8 percent; and International Stores, 3.2 percent. At the end of the 1970s, Sainsbury emerged as the leading grocery firm with a market share of 13.4 percent, followed by Tesco at 13.4 percent, ASDA at 8.5 percent, Fine Fare at 5.5 percent, Kwik Save at 5.4 percent, and International Stores at 4.7 percent. This trend in concentration can be explained by the expansion of the market share of leading firms in the industry. An important motive for increasing market share appears to have been the desire to extract better terms from suppliers. Fierce competition and increasing market power with large retailers seem to have created fear among consumers, though gross margins of retailers have fallen and consumers have benefited from competition.[8]

As in the United States, there has been a swing back toward smaller specialty stores in fashion apparel in Germany and the United Kingdom. In line with this trend, one of the leading German department stores, Hertie, recently opened a unique store, the Ziel, on Frankfurt's main shopping street, which is designed to project the appearance of a collection of high-quality specialty shops rather than a typical department store.[9] The U.K. retail market presents several instances of 'upmarketing' product image by leading chains. Chelsea Girl, traditionally a women's store, is looking for more sophistication and style. It has recently decided to include a men's section and to push the products slightly upmarket toward the over-twenties age group. Austin Reed, a major British clothes designer, is moving in a similar direction.[10] The trend toward smaller size of retail establishment has been caused by several factors. Pressure for higher retail productivity in the wake of current inflationary trends is one major reason why investors are backing away from 'superdepartment stores' and big shopping complexes. High square footage rates have made shopping complexes an unviable proposition. Besides the cost, another important factor is the changing consumer profile. Younger buyers seem to be more quality and service conscious and are overwhelmed, even confused, by the endless variations of similar products, a marketing phenomenon that the British F. W. Woolworth probably failed to comprehend and respond to.[11]

The pace of modernization has been relatively slow in France and Italy, where retailing facilities are still widely scattered and independently owned. Although France has a few large retail companies with large distribution networks, these are mostly located in northern France. According to a 1969 survey carried out by the Italian National Institute for Distribution, 40 percent of Italian retail shops had less than 24 square meters of sales area, only 10 percent had a cash register, and the average number of employees was slightly above two.

Though the survey findings are quite old now, the Italian retailing is still dominated largely by small independent stores, far behind in modernization compared to other European countries. Subsequent studies, for example, showed that only 3 percent of retail grocery trade in Italy was accounted for by corporate chains. Thirty percent of grocery stores in Italy sold frozen foods, compared to 34 percent in France, 51 percent in Belgium and 85 percent in Netherlands. The proportion of grocery stores selling stationery and textiles was also the lowest in Italy.[12]

Regarding installing computerized inventory control and check-out systems, retail stores in many European countries are still far behind their U.S. counterparts. Next to the United States, however, Germany has the largest number of retail stores with optical scanners in the world. Based on reports of the International Article Numbering Association, the number of stores with optical scanners as of September 1981 varied in various European countries as follows: Germany, 38; France, 11; Sweden, 11; Italy, 10; Switzerland, 9; U.K., 8; Austria, 3; Netherlands, 3; Norway, 2; and Belgium, 1.[13]

For many years, European retailing borrowed new strategies and techniques, primarily from the United States, to enhance productivity and its competitive edge. Many institutional frameworks and operating systems that had been successful in the United States moved gradually across the Atlantic. Nevertheless, some innovative ideas have originated in Europe. First, the institution of the downtown department store was founded in Europe, though it remains a controversial issue whether Au Bon Marche, the French department store, is the world's oldest department store. The roots of Bon Marche were developed as early as 1838 when it was a small dry-goods store. A few years later, De Bijenkorf came into existence in Amsterdam in the form of a small variety store. Department stores appeared in the United States about the same time, but their merchandise mix was not as comprehensive as that of the French Bon Marche or the British Whiteley's.[14]

Second, Europe could boast of no-frill box stores with a limited number of items, which were founded by famous grocery chains like Aldi and Tengelmann in Germany, presumably during the postwar period. Albrecht KG, the owner of Aldi stores, introduced limited-range grocery stores even in the United States through its subsidiary Aldi-Benner. This institution was unique in the sense that the customers could buy all essential items without any frill—no price tags and no shopping bag—at considerably reduced discount prices, thus meeting the challenge of the galloping inflation that swept Germany during the postwar period.

Another form of retail institution that emerged in Europe in the mid-1960s in response to inflationary trends was the price club or warehouse club, which originated in Europe as giant wholesale supermarkets for small food and drug retailers. A warehouse club, as one reporter described it, "ignores nearly every rule of successful marketing. It has a lousy location and looks ugly. It carries a limited number of brands—only the top sellers. It doesn't provide customers with service and doesn't accept credit cards. It does little advertising—all the warehouse club does is sell."[15] The key to its survival is low pricing and a loyal membership of wholesale and retail customers. Its average markup is 10 percent (most other retailers markup 20 percent to 50 percent). The concept began to catch on in the United States in 1976; the number of warehouse outlets and sales there jumped between 1979 and 1983, reaching an annual turnover of $700 million in 1983.

The concept of the hypermarket originated in Europe in 1962 and beat all records of large-scale retailing. The first hypermarket was set up in Belgium by the well-known GB group. A hypermarket is a huge self-service retail outlet covering a sales area of 2,500 square meters or more with a large number of check-outs. It sells all categories of consumer goods: grocery, soft lines, and hard lines including furniture, garden equipment, home construction material, and auto parts. The sales area is generally divided between food and nonfood items in the ratio of 60:40. A much larger-size sales area extending up to 20,000 square meters with parking facilities for over 3,000 cars is not uncommon. Some of these large hypermarkets warehouse the merchandise right in the sales area on upper shelves. The huge size of the retail operation allows scale economies in several functions, such as purchasing, inventory control, energy consumption, deployment of personnel, and construction and maintenance.[16]

Thus, the institution of the hypermarket epitomized two major retailing innovations adopted earlier in Europe: self-service and discounting. According to the sixteenth census of hypermarkets in Germany, there were 821 hypermarkets, of which 123 claimed a selling space of 10,000 square meters or more.[17] GB's novel venture was the forerunner of similar efforts in many other countries, notably France and West Germany. Carrefour, the leading French retailer established in 1959, operates 53 hypermarkets in France. Its Brazilian subsidiary, Tervo, operates eight hypermarkets in that country and one in Argentina. Carrefour also has minority-owned operations in Great Britain, Italy, and Switzerland. Promodes and Docks De France, other French companies, operated, respectively, 28 and 35 hypermarkets at the end of 1981. Among other leading companies in this field, mention should be made of Delhaize Le Lion in Belgium, KBB,

Vroom & Dreesmann, and Ahold in the Netherlands, and Tengelmann and the Hugo Mann Group of West Germany. Sweden's giant KF Cooperative also set up hypermarkets in Scandinavia. The hypermarket concept has been tried in the United States by Jewel Grand Bazar in Chicago and Meijers Thrifty Acres in Michigan, with limited success.[18]

Another landmark in the history of European retailing was reached when the Oetker group of Germany, a leading producer of foodstuffs and drinks, signed an agreement in 1981 with the Polish state organization Pewex to open retail shops for its products in Poland.[19] Such collaborations are expected to continue and will gradually bridge the commercial gap between the two blocs.

Thus, the retailing industry in Europe has undergone several structural changes during the past two decades, especially since the formation of the EEC. Despite the political pull that small retailers enjoyed in many countries, most have faced up to the need to change or go out of business. Several patterns of integration emerged among the small single-line retailers in response to the arrival of large-scale retailing in Europe. In most countries, the size of the average retail firm increased, though moves toward bigger shopping centers and stores were constrained by costs and state regulation. This development led to an increase in the bargaining power of European retailers. It enabled them to initiate independent marketing programs, develop private labels, and seek better business terms from suppliers. Simultaneously the European marketplace witnessed several retailing innovations—self-service food stores, combination stores, no-frill box stores, price clubs, and hypermarkets—that revolutionized both small- and large-scale retailing on the continent. There has been an increasing trend toward mail-order buying and the use of computerized business systems, especially in Scandinavian countries, the United Kingdom, the Benelux, and Germany.

European countries not only rebuilt their manufacturing facilities during the postwar period, particularly during the preceding two decades, but also did an excellent job of rebuilding and revitalizing the retailing infrastructure. Many enterprising retail companies in France, Germany, and the Netherlands diversified their operations over a wide spectrum ranging from small convenience stores to hypermarkets. Some of these companies extended their operations to overseas markets and made sizable investments in the U.S. retail business.

NOTES

1. Angus Hone and Andreas Schlapfer, *Marketing in Europe* (Geneva: International Trade Center, UNCTAD/GATT, 1974).

2. Michel David, "Developments in the Structure of Distribution in France, A Modest Degree of Concentration," *Journal of Retailing* (Summer 1965): 34-44.

3. "A Supermarket without a Store," *Business Week*, January 11, 1964, pp. 100-102.

4. For a lucid and detailed account of integrative trends in Scandinavian retailing, see A. Leonides Trotta, ed., *Retailing International, 1969-1970* (New York: National Retail Merchants Association, 1969), pp. 60-69, 101-109.

5. Ibid., p. 68.

6. Hone and Schlapfer, *Marketing*.

7. "British Food Marketing—The Winning Ways of Brand X," *Economist*, September 4, 1982, p. 72.

8. C. W. F. Baden Fuller, "Rising Concentration: Are Fears Justified?" in *The U.K. Grocery Trade 1970-80*, Research in Marketing Series (London: London Business School, July 1982).

9. "West German Retailing—Upmarket on Downhill," *Economist*, July 2, 1983, p. 64.

10. "The Changing Face of Marketing," *Marketing*, December 1, 1983, p. 30, and "Austin Reed Gears toward the 20 Year Old Male," *Marketing*, November 24, 1983, p. 18.

11. "Gloom for Shopping Complexes," *Marketing*, December 16, 1982, p. 8.

12. J. Dawson, "Retail Trends in the E.E.C." in Ross L. Davies, ed., *Retail Planning in the European Community* (Farnborough, England: Gower Publishing Company, 1979), pp. 32 and 40.

13. "The Progress of Scanning," *Retailing Today* (July 1982): 2.

14. For a more detailed argument against Bon Marche's claim as the world's oldest department store, see Ralph M. Hower, *History of Macy's of New York, 1858-1919*" (Cambridge: Harvard University Press, 1943), pp. 72, 413.

15. "Big Warehouse Outlets Break Traditional Rules of Retailing," *Wall Street Journal*, December 22, 1983, p. 27.

16. For details, see J. A. Dawson, "Structural-Spatial Relationships in the Spread of Hypermarket Retailing," in E. Kaynak and R. Savitt, eds., *Comparative Marketing Systems* (New York: Praeger, 1984).

17. "International Association of Department Stores," *Retail News Letter* (Paris) (July 1981): 8.

18. William R. Davidson, Albert D. Bates, and Stephen J. Bass, "The Retail Life Cycle," *Harvard Business Review* (November-December 1976): 93.

19. "International Association of Department Stores," *Retail News Letter* (Paris) (November 1981): 12.

3

Trends in Foreign Direct Investment in U.S. Retailing

Retailing travels slow, they used to say. It is one of the essential marketing services that every individual, family, and organization needs. Goods and services normally bought may satisfy more than economic needs. There are also social, sociopsychological, and cultural dimensions of human needs that no retail enterprise can afford to ignore. It is these extraeconomic dimensions of human needs that make the complexion of retailing different from region to region and country to country. Thus, retailing has remained by and large a local phenomenon, staffed by local people and consummated in accord with local culture, traditions, and preferences.

The need for maintaining a local character and conforming to local values and norms, however, has not deterred some reputable retail houses from venturing into other countries to set up branches or subsidiaries. Woolworth made its first international venture into Canada as early as 1907, and Sears, Roebuck set up its first foreign corporation in Cuba in 1942. Thus, Woolworth and Sears, Roebuck offer two leading examples of strategic international expansion of American retailers. Among manufacturers, Bata Shoe Organization, headquartered in Toronto, Canada, and the Singer Company, headquartered in the United States, are considered to be among the pioneers of specialty retail chains, having set up hundreds of company-owned or franchised retail stores virtually all over the world.

There are also small clusters of famous specialty chains located in leading world cities—Paris, London, New York, Los Angeles, Tokyo—such as Gucci, Roberta, Dunhill, and Brooks. Pringles, a Scotland-based manufacturer of fine sweaters, owns retail shops in Amsterdam, Vienna, and Dusseldorf. Among jewelers and art dealers, the names of H. Stern, Van Cleef & Arpels, Spritzer & Furham, Wildenstein & Co., Christie's, London Graphics, and M. K. Knoedler are well known. They have set up a limited number of operations in selected metropolitan centers, mostly in Europe and North and South America, making retailing a global phenomenon.[1]

This intercontinental trend accelerated with an increase in retailing partnerships between Western and Oriental business firms. For example, the famous Japanese retail company, Daiei, Inc., today owns a discount chain in Honolulu. The leading retail stores of Japan—Matsuzukiya, Mikimoto, and Takashimaya—have been operating in Los Angeles and New York for several years. Sears, Roebuck has a longstanding management contract with Tokyo's leading department store chain, Seibu. Safeway also has a similar management contract to run leading supermarkets in Saudi Arabia.

In recent years, there has been an increasing flow of foreign direct investment in the trade sector in the United States that has significantly affected the retail industry. The trend is important for several reasons. One is the scale of the international retailing. Never before have so many European countries been seriously interested in making investments in and controlling U.S. retail companies. The trend signifies a reverse flow—a type of economic rebuttal from Europe, which has been on the receiving end for so many years. The new trend represents a serious interest in overseas retailing. Though still relatively small, the volume of foreign investments in various food and nonfood sectors of the U.S. retail trade has mounted steadily over the past ten years.

The history of foreign companies' involvement in U.S. retailing in an organized way dates back to 1939 when Loblaw Companies, Ltd., Canada (controlled by George Weston Ltd., Canada), established Loblaw, Inc., a food store chain in the United States with stores concentrated in New York, Pennsylvania, and Ohio. In 1955-1956, the same Canadian parent acquired National Tea Company, with stores in Chicago, New Orleans, St. Louis, Indianapolis, Milwaukee, Minneapolis, Denver, and Davenport. About six years later, a French company, Schlumberger, Ltd., acquired Heath Company, a do-it-yourself electronic kits retailer in 1962, and Julio Tanjeloff of Argentina acquired Astro Minerals, Ltd., a New York-based gems and precious stones retailer in 1963. The Dutch family Brenninkmeyer acquired Ohrbach's, a ready-to-wear apparel retailer, in 1965, an eleven-store chain in New York and California.

RECENT TRENDS

U.S. Department of Commerce publications provide limited data on foreign direct investments in retail trade separately. Most of the time, data on retail trade are lumped together with general data on trade sector. Investments in trade sector have registered a steady increase since the mid-1970s, as will be seen from tables 3.1 and 3.2 which bear out the fact that the volume of direct investments registered a four-fold increase since 1976. The period 1979 through 1982 witnessed a spectacular growth of about 80 percent.

Table 3.1
Foreign Direct Investment in the Trade Sector

Year	Volume (million $)	Rate of Growth (%)
1976	6,123	
1977	7,237	18
1978	9,161	27
1979	11,562	26
1980	14,296	24
1981	17,628	23
1982	20,630	17

SOURCE: U.S. Department of Commerce, *Survey of Current Business* (Washington, D.C.: Government Printing Office, various years).

The volume of foreign investments in retail trade is a substantial part of the total volume in trade sector, though not as big as that of wholesale trade. Table 3.2, based on the data published recently by the U.S. Department of Commerce, bears this out and shows a consistent improvement in the position of foreign direct investments in retail trade.

Table 3.2
Foreign Direct Investment Position in U.S. in Trade Sector (Millions of dollars)

Year	Volume in trade sector*	Volume in wholesale trade	Volume in retail trade	Volume of investments in retail trade shared by European countries	Percentage share
1980	15,210	11,560	3,650	3,029	83
1981	19,739	15,501	4,238	3,541	84
1982	22,656	17,699	4,957	4,015	81
1983	25,058	20,006	5,052	4,084	81

SOURCE: U.S. Department of Commerce, *Survey of Current Business* (Washington, D.C.: Government Printing Office, October 1984).

*The data on foreign direct investments in trade sector in table 3.1 do not match those in table 3.2, from 1980 onwards, due to major changes in data collection procedures.

According to data published by the Department of Commerce, International Trade Administration division, the number of completed transactions in retail trade increased from 26 in 1977 to 53 in 1980 and fell to 44 in 1981.[2] The annual sales of U.S. affiliates of foreign companies in retail trade, which stood at 5.6 billion in 1974, rose to $7.6 billion in 1977 and $19.3 billion in 1980, and are estimated to be around $30 billion in 1982.[3] No doubt, the sales volume is still very small considering the magnitude of total sales of the retail industry, which became a trillion-dollar industry in 1981. Still, the share of foreign U.S. affiliates falls in the range of 3 percent and would be estimated as higher, probably to 5 percent, if some nonrelevant sectors of the retail trade (unaffected by foreign direct investments) are excluded, such as building materials and automotive dealers.

According to Department of Commerce economists, foreign investors control more than 24 major retail and food service chains with a combined sales approximating $30 billion. A major part of this investment has occurred since 1976. It is estimated that the continuation of this trend would put 25 percent of the U.S. food market in the hands of the Canadians, Belgians, British, French, and West Germans by the mid-1980s. Foreign companies own 14 U.S. grocery firms outright and hold partial ownership in 9 others according to economists N. Seigle and C. Handy. The 1979 sales of these firms totaled $19 billion—about 11 percent of the total grocery store sales in the United States for that year.[4]

Next to grocery stores, specialty chains and variety store chains have become attractive to foreign investors. Many European corporations are believed to have allocated between $200 million and $400 million for the purchase of specialty retail chains.[5] Some of the better-known acquisitions of specialty chains are F.A.O. Schwartz (toys), Ohrbach's (fashion apparel), and Mother-to-Be (maternity apparel).

A dominant characteristic of foreign ownership in U.S. retailing is that in most cases the foreign companies have acquired an ongoing retail operation rather than establishing a new setup in the United States. One noteworthy exception is Habitat, the London-based home furnishing chain, which entered the U.S. market with its unique life-style retailing under the name Conran's. Contrary to the general trend, most U.S. companies—Sears, Woolworth, Safeway, Singer and Tandy—made direct investments abroad, carrying with them their retailing models and establishing new stores.

Among the countries participating in foreign investments in the retail trade, the United Kingdom and Canada generally have been at the top, followed by West Germany, the Netherlands, France, Switzerland, and Japan (not necessarily in that order). This is evidenced in table 3.3, which presents direct investment distribution of U.S. affiliates in retail trade by country of foreign parent. The significant role played by European Countries is also evidenced in table 3.2. Interestingly, OPEC countries have not taken much interest in making direct investments in the U.S. retail industry. In 1980 and 1981, there was only one instance of such an investment between January and June 1981.[6] Sheik Mohammad-al-Fassi

Table 3.3
Direct Investment Distribution of U.S. Affiliates in Retail Trade
by Country of Foreign Parent

	Total	Canada	France	Japan	Nether-lands	Switzer-land	United Kingdom	West Germany	All Others
1979									
Total no./cases	45	8	3	9	2	0	6	9	8
Value ($ million)	212.3	36.6	48.7	0.5	16.0		3.6	94.7	12.2
1980									
Total no./cases	53	11	5	5	3	1	9	9	10
Value ($ million)	1,047	127.1	23.0	15.3	25.4	10.0	742.2	67.9	36.3
1981									
Total no./cases	44	5	0	5	4	6	11	4	9
Value ($ million)	659.3	183.9	0.0	3.5	89.0	7.0	161.6	122.0	92.3

SOURCE: *Foreign Direct Investment in the United States,* U.S. Department of Commerce, International Trade Administration, Washington D.C., U.S. Government Printing Office, September 1980, October 1981 and December 1982.

from Saudi Arabia showed some interest in acquiring the chain of 336 Woolco stores, which Woolworth had decided to close in early 1983. The sheik, however, decided against acquiring.

It is not possible to provide specific data on increases or losses in employment in retail firms in which direct investments were made by overseas companies. According to one estimate made by the Department of Commerce, the foreign-owned companies as a whole employed about 2 percent of all business employment in the United States; within this small slice, the level of employment was believed to be rising by 3 percent per year between 1974 and 1977, compared to a 1.6 percent rise in the employment in the domestic companies during the same period.[7] Within the retail sector, the employment level in foreign-owned U.S. affiliates rose from an estimated 96,735 in 1975 to 129,097 in 1977, 226,756 in 1979, and 334,383 in 1981.[8] Table 3.4 presents some information on financial performance and employment in these affiliates for recent years.

Table 3.4
Sales, Net Income, and Employment of U.S. Affiliates of
Foreign Companies in the Retail Trade

	1980	1981	1982 (Estimated)
Sales (million)	23,577	26,907	29,600
Net income (million)	278	326	360
Employment	304,380	334,383	393,000

SOURCE: Department of Commerce, *Survey of Current Business* (Washington, D.C.: Government Printing Office, various years).

The data reflect a significant trend in international retailing. The seriousness of the situation, however, seems to be greater than what is reflected from statistics. It is noteworthy that some of the flagstores of this country—the historic A&P, the glamorous Saks Fifth Avenue and Ohrbach's, the leading discounter Korvettes, and lately the pride of Chicago, Marshall Field—have gone to European ownership. Table 3.5 presents important data on major acquisitions of U.S. retail firms by European companies during the 1970s and early 1980s. Parts A and B of this table present selected data on leading foreign companies which made investments in the U.S. retail business until 1975. Data for subsequent years follow in Part C. Figures 3.1 to 3.4 illustrate the trends discussed in this chapter.

Table 3.5
Overview of Major Retail Acquisitions

(A) Pre-1975 Situation

Name of U.S. Company	Foreign Owner	Country	Ownership	Type of Stores	Estimates Sales in 1975 (millions)	Estimated Employment	Rank
1. Brown & Williamson	British American Tobacco	U.K.	100%	Department stores & supermarkets	2,600	40,000	2
2. Grand Union	Generale Occidentale S.A.	France	100	Supermarkets	1,611	21,000	4
3. National Tea	George Weston	Canada	84	Supermarkets	1,472	18,000	5
4. Loblaw Inc.	George Weston	Canada	100	Supermarkets	481	4,000	23
5. Kay Corp.	Bowater Corp.	U.K.	72	Retail jewelry stores	242	1,310	46
6. Ohrbach's	Brennink-meyer	Netherlands	100	Department stores	150	2,500	65
7. Bond Industry	Seamer NV	Netherlands	54	Apparel	99	3,625	87

Table 3.5 (continued)

(B) Pre-1975 with Lower Ranks

Year of Investment	Name of U.S. Company	Foreign Owner	Country	Ownership	Type of Stores	1981 Sales (millions)	1981 Net Income (millions)	1981 Assets (millions)	Size of Investment (millions)
1. 1973	F.A.O. Schwartz	Franz Carl Weber	Switzerland	100%	Toys	20.0	n.a.	n.a.	$3
2. 1974	Baskin Robbins	J. Lyons & Co.	U.K.	100	Ice cream	300.0	n.a.	n.a.	n.a.
3. 1975	Food Town Stores	Establishments Delhaize Freres	Belgium	52	Supermarket	667.0	19.3	139	27
4. 1975	Fed Mart Corp.	Hugo Mann Group	Federal Republic of Germany	88	Discount chain	1061.0	6.3	321	21.5

(C) Pre-1976-1984 Situation

Year of Investment	Name of U.S. Company	Foreign Owner	Country	Ownership	Type of Stores	1981 Sales (millions)	1981 Net Income (millions)	1981 Assets (millions)	Size of initial Investment (millions)
1. 1976	Mother-to-Be (Dekon)	Mothercare PLC (Now Habitat Mothercare)	U.K.	100%	Maternity chain	$28	n.a.	n.a.	$1
2. 1976	Benner Tea Co.	Albrecht Group	Germany	100	Grocery	30	n.a.	n.a.	n.a.

3. 1977	Scrivner	Franz Haniel & Cie	Germany	100	Wholesale, retail, food, and department stores	864	9.7	121	27.7
4. 1977	Bi-Lo	Ahold N.V.	Netherlands	100	Supermarket	728	25 (1979)	n.a.	60
5. 1978	Maurice's	Brennikmeyer C & A	Netherlands	100	Clothing	n.a.	n.a.	n.a.	n.a.
6. 1978	Lil-Champ	Docks De France	France	35	Convenience stores	37.6	1.3	13.4	3
7. 1979	Dillard	Vroom & Dreesmann	Netherlands	52	Department stores	593	16.3	344	35
8. 1979	Outlet Stores	Vroom & Dreesmann	Netherlands		Department stores	132	-37	n.a.	n.a.
9. 1979	Cole Corp.	Vroom & Dreesmann	Netherlands	14	Variety of retail operations	174	6.7	168	3.75
10. 1979	H. J. Wilson	Vroom & Dreesmann	Netherlands	21	Catalog stores	403	12.7	321	12
11. 1979	Korvettes	Agache-Willot	France	100	Discount department stores	600	(5.4)	n.a.	55
12. 1979	A&P	Tengelmann	Germany	50	Supermarket	6,227	31.6	1,142	80
13. 1979	Winn's	Heinrich Bauer Verlag	Germany	100	Variety stores	73.1	4.8	n.a.	50
14. 1980	Red Food	Promodes	France	100	Supermarket	313	5.9	n.a.	36
15. 1980	Food Giant (Alterman Food)	Delhaize Le Lion	Belgium	100	Supermarket	591	-2.8	71	36
16. 1980	Macks	KBB	Netherlands	51	Variety stores	62.4	1.4	23	15

Table 3.5 *(continued)*

Year of Investment	Name of U.S. Company	Foreign Owner	Country	Ownership	Type of Stores	1981 Sales (millions)	1981 Net Income (millions)	1981 Assets (millions)	Size of initial Investment (millions)
17. 1980	Albertson's	Albrecht	Germany	6.6	Supermarket	3,480	48	709	18
18. 1980	Intercontinental	Grand Metropolitan	U.K.	100	Hotel chain	269	25.4	277	n.a.
19. 1980	Howard Johnson	Imperial Group	U.K.	100	Hotel chain	699	n.a.	n.a.	630
20. 1980	Holiday Mart (Honolulu)	Dai-ei	Japan	100	Discount store chain	n.a.	n.a.	n.a.	15
21. 1981	Harris Co.	El Corte Ingleo	Spain	100	Department store	n.a.	n.a.	n.a.	9
22. 1981	Giant Foods	Ahold N.V.	Netherlands	100	Supermarket	300	n.a.	n.a.	35
23. 1981	Marshall Field	Batus Inc. (Subsidiary of BAT)	U.K.	80	Department store	1,194	22.6	681	310
24. 1981	Spiegel Inc.	Otto Versand	Germany	100	Catalog store	423	1.7	441	over 50
25. 1983	Shaw's Supermarkets	Sainsbury	United Kingdom	21	Supermarkets	700 (1983)	n.a.	n.a.	20.1
26. 1984	Thriftmart Inc.	Casino Group	France	majority	Cash & carry outlets	502.9 (1983)	5.04 (1983)	98.6 (1983)	n.a.
27. 1984	Guiland, Athlete's Foot	Rallye	France	67	Sporting goods chain	200 (1983)	n.a.	n.a.	n.a.
28. 1984	Fanny Farmer	Poulain	France	100	Confectionary retail chain	53 (1984)	n.a.	n.a.	12.8

SOURCES: Across the Board, December 1976, pp. 21-29. Annual reports of European parent companies; annual reports of U.S. affiliates; *Forbes,* July 5, 1982, pp. 115-126; *Fortune,* December 1, 1980.

Figure 3.1
Foreign Direct Investment in the U.S. Trade Sector

BILLIONS $US

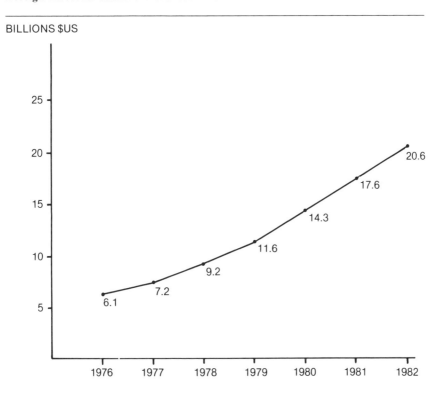

Figure 3.2
Number of Completed Foreign Direct Investment Transactions in the Retail Trade Sector

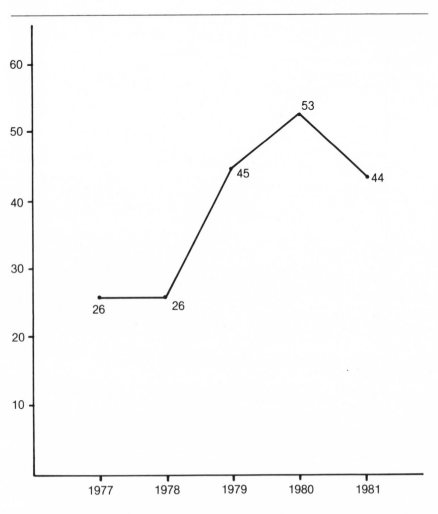

Figure 3.3
Sales of U.S. Affiliates of Foreign Companies in Retail Trade

BILLIONS $US

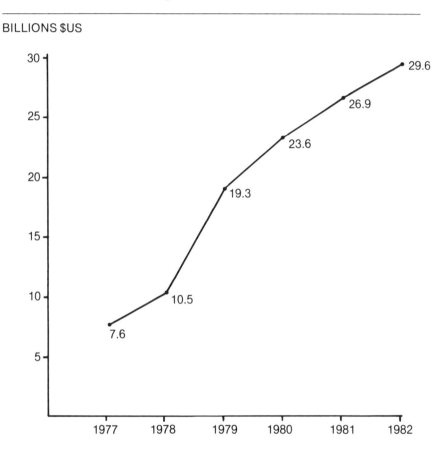

Figure 3.4
Number of Employees in Foreign-Controlled U.S. Retail Companies

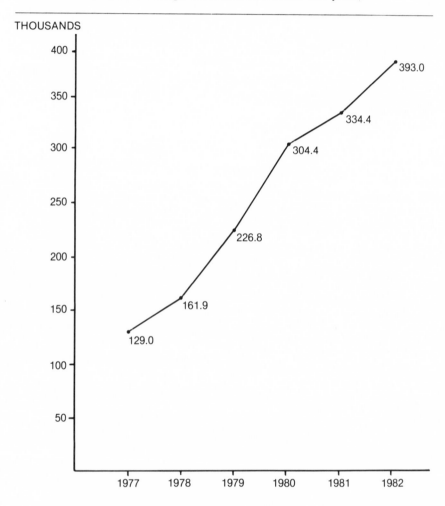

NOTES

1. For an excellent discussion on the growth of international retailing and the gradual spread of specialty shops in major metropolitan centers of the world, see Stanley C. Hollander, *Multinational Retailing*, MSU International Business and Economic Studies, Michigan State University, East Lansing, 1970, pp. 14-54.

2. U. S. Department of Commerce, International Trade Administration, *Foreign Direct Investments in the United States, 1980 and 1981 Transactions* (Washington, D.C.: Government Printing Office, October 1981, December 1982).

3. "Selected Data on the Operations of U. S. Affiliates of Foreign Companies, 1977," *Survey of Current Business* (July 1980): 36, (May 1981): 43-44, (November 1983): 24-25.

4. Ken Rankin, "Who's Buying What," *Chain Store Age Executive* (August 1981): 10; also see *Feedstuffs*, October 19, 1981, p. 8.

5. "European Target Specialty Chains," *Chain Store Age Executive* (January 1982): 68-69.

6. U.S. Department of Commerce, Office of International Investment, *OPEC Direct Investment in the United States* (Washington, D. C.: Government Printing Office, 1981), p. 12. *Wall Street Journal*, October 5, 1982, p. 24.

7. U. S. Department of Commerce, International Trade Administration, *Attracting Foreign Investment to the United States* (Washington, D.C.: Government Printing Office, 1981), pp. 1-18.

8. "Selected Data on the Operations of U. S. Affiliates of Foreign Companies," op. cit. (June 1983): 31, (November 1983): 20, 24-25.

4

Profiles of Major European Investors

TENGELMANN GROUP

The Tengelmann Group is a family-owned West German retailer; it is a private company and not obligated to publish its financial results. It is accepted as a solid business house with tremendous resources and an excellent in-house source of capital. According to Henry W. Van Baalan, Tengelmann's U.S. representative, the chief executives of this group have enjoyed the reputation of builders and developers. Erivan Haub, the present chief executive, has been known for innovative thinking and risk taking. He owns 50 percent of Tengelmann; the rest of it is owned by his sons. He is no stranger to the United States or to the supermarket wars being waged in this country. During the 1950s, Haub worked for the Chicago-based Jewel Company and California's Alpha Beta chain. He also worked in the field of real estate and banking in Germany before joining the Tengelmann Group in 1963 as a district manager.[1]

The group owns around 2,000 grocery and limited-range discount stores in Germany and Austria. Many of these stores were acquired and made financially sound. The limited-range discount stores, called Plus stores, generally offer fewer than 1,000 items, sold at discounts up to 30 percent. In 1978-1979, these stores accounted for sales of $2.6 billion. As far as product lines are concerned, stress is laid on gourmet food lines and in-shop butchers and bakers. In 1971, the Tengelmann Group purchased Kaiser's, one of the largest German grocery chains with sales of $713 million. This chain has more than 500 stores, 5 hypermarkets, 217 supermarkets, and 74 drugstores.[2]

Tengelmann is one of the four largest retail chains of Germany (the others are Aldi, Coop, and Leibbrand). These chains control about 33 percent of the German market, a share expected to increase to 36 percent by 1985, according to K. Wiegandt, general manager of Leibbrand.[3] Tengelmann has invested over $100 million in the company. Like other retailers in Europe, the Tengelmann Group felt that it was running out of space in West Germany. It acquired 50.3 percent ownership in the A&P in 1979 and has invested over $100 million in it.

Tengelmann's biggest German competitor is Albrecht KG, the owner of Aldi, which through its subsidiary Aldi-Benner Inc. introduced limited-range grocery stores in the United States.

HUGO MANN GROUP

Hugo Mann is considered to be one of the most successful entrepreneurs in the Federal Republic of Germany. He made a remarkable contribution to the postwar development of German retail trade. Starting as a small furniture business in 1950, the Mann enterprises, mainly Wertkauf Centers and Mann Mobilia, account for annual sales of approximately DM 3.0 billion. These enterprises introduced the self-service principle in the hard goods sector in Europe more than twenty years ago. The principle turned out to be a breakthrough in this sector and changed the image of Hugo Mann from one of hard discounter to that of an operator of the most modern self-service chain.

Initially Mann limited his activities to southwest Germany. After operating for about 25 years in this area, he began to expand by taking over and building commercial enterprises in the North Rhine-Westphalia and Hamburg areas. In the early seventies, he began exploring the U.S. market, which led to the acquisition of a major shareholding in Fed Mart, a self-service department store in the Southwest United States in the summer of 1975. In Germany, the expansion of Wertkauf stores drew country-wide attention in 1977 when the company opened ten completely refurbished stores at the same hour on the same day.

After the Wertkauf Centers proved successful, Mann pioneered a new concept of living through his furniture chain, Mann Mobilia, which opened in 1970. "In these furniture and accessory furnishing centers, everything directly associated with the quality of life is sold—from books to bed linens, from T.V. sets to towels, from furniture to precious china, from oriental rugs to works of graphic art."[4] The concept, which appealed to young families, took off successfully. Since 1975, sales outlets of Mann Mobilia have spread over 14 places between Düsseldorf and Stuttgart.

Surpassing even the conventional discount stores, Mann outlets rely on quick turnover and high volume. The stores are equipped with electronic check-out machines hooked into a central computer system. The sales area of a typical Wertkauf hypermarket is 18,000 square meters, allocated to grocery (around 40 percent) and nongrocery items (around 60 percent), which include soft merchandise, garden equipment, auto service center, tires, washers, dry-cleaning services, a cafeteria, fancy jewelery, newspapers, cigarettes, and leather goods. A large hypermarket provides parking space for over 3,000 cars. One distinctive feature of hypermarkets is in-store warehousing; the merchandise remains stored within the respective departments on the upper shelves and moves down as merchandise on the lower shelves is sold. Another related feature is that all merchandise comes directly to the store from manufacturers and suppliers without being routed through a warehouse.

In 1975, the Hugo Mann Group made its first entry in the U.S. market by negotiating a deal to acquire 68 percent of the stock of Fed Mart—a West Coast chain of 48 supermarkets and general merchandise stores—for $20 million. In 1977, the group bought a huge chunk of Vornado Inc., owner of 140 Two Guys discount outlets and the Builders Emporium home repair centers. In 1979, the Mann Group was fairly optimistic about the possibility of converting some of the Fed Mart stores into hypermarkets in the San Diego region. Heinz Gundlach, Fed Mart's vice-chairman, expressed such hopes earlier in 1977 when he said that their first hypermarket would open in San Diego by year end. In 1981, however, the company decided to wind up its retailing operations in the United States.[5]

VROOM & DREESMANN

A Dutch-based privately held retailing company, Vroom & Dreesmann engages in a diverse range of business activities in Holland, the United States, Japan, and Brazil. Headquartered in Amsterdam and based in a small country of 14 million inhabitants, the company had to seek growth by moving outside its country as well as its core business activity, retailing. It entered commercial banking and a wide assortment of other services, such as providing temporary help, cleaning office buildings, renting linens, catering, operating an international express service for small packages, and cable television. Even in retailing, it branched out from its traditional department store base to food discounting and specialty shops in hard and soft goods fields. At an estimated sales volume of over $3.5 billion, Vroom & Dressmann is bigger than C&A in Holland and larger than the two publicly quoted Dutch retailers, Bijenkorf and Ahold. The group not only holds a dominant position in the country's retail trade; its yearly rate of growth exceeds by far that of the Dutch economy as a whole.

Certain environmental developments in Holland—curbs on consumer credit, tough planning laws, lagging consumer expenditure, high interest rates, overstoring, and rising price competition—prevented the opening of new stores during the late sixties and early seventies and forced Vroom & Dreesmann to scrap plans for a much-needed expansion of their Amsterdam city-center store. Its 1978-1979 profits were $50 million, up by only 19 percent compared with 35 percent profit growth in 1977-1978.[6]

Vroom & Dreesmann has been far more adventurous in pursuing a strong strategy of international expansion than the three competitors they encounter in the Netherlands. The group maintains an organizational style that responds rapidly to unexpected opportunities and eliminates delays and rigidity.

Vroom & Dreesmann outlined their business strategies as follows:

1. To strengthen existing commercial activities by increased efforts directed at moving market sectors through creative merchandising, remodeling of stores, and diligent improvement of store locations and by keeping an innovative and orderly organizational structure, short communication lines, and motivated employees.
2. To diversify into promising market sectors and geographical areas, such as mail-order, financial services, and other international markets.[7]

The group adopted a general rule that about 60 percent of future investments will be made in the Netherlands and surrounding European areas and the balance in international markets, mainly in the United States, Brazil, and Japan.

The commercial organization of Vroom & Dreesmann consists of eight divisions: general merchandise, soft goods, hard goods, food, mail order, financial services, services, and international.

General Merchandise Division

The division consists of Vroom & Dreesmann's traditional department stores, Vendet Junior Department stores, Van Reeuwijk and Vendomus furniture and home decorating stores, SuperDoe Home centers, and In de Lanscroon wine and liquor stores.

The department store chain is organized into eleven regions, each region having its own distribution center. Unlike the United States, European department stores have traditionally emphasized food and other nontextile merchandise and thus remained weak in fashion goods, such as ladies' ready-to-wear items. A long-term program is underway to rejuvenate the department stores' fashion image. Some of the Vendet Junior stores are being upgraded into full-line department stores, and the restaurants are being converted into self-service operations. The group's strength in this area is as follows: automated distribution center, sophisticated electronic data processing, a high degree of creativity in buying and selling, and adaptation to high-tech merchandise. Although the department store as a retail outlet is gradually drifting toward decline, the group has been trying to preserve and revitalize this form of distribution.

The Van Reeuwijk chain of furniture and home decorating stores was added to the group during 1981-1982. The chain operates ten units; its largest store, in Rotterdam, is a leader in the field of soft furnishings and quality furniture. Although currently experiencing severe internal and environmental problems, the group is confident that by renovating and reorganizing, the chain will be successful.

Soft Goods Division

The division consists of several retail clothing chains, most of them operated under a franchise system by independent businessmen. Affected adversely by shrinking disposable income, some components of this division, especially those selling durable goods such as men's suits and winter coats, remained hard-pressed during 1980-1982. The performance of some chains in this division—Kreymborg (ladies' and men's apparel), Hunkemoller (foundation garments), and Claudia Strater (high fashion ladies' apparel)—was considered to be relatively better during this period.

Hard Goods Division

This division consists of many recent additions to the Vroom & Dreesmann organization, such as Kijkshop (showroom retailing), Dixons (photo, hi-fi, electronics, and records), consumer electronics and home appliance stores such as Rovato, Guco, Heijmans, and Electro-Jacobs, Rinck (opticians), Siebel (jewelers), Peek Yachting International, and Vendoto automotive shops.

Food Division

A variety of enterprises form parts of this division: Edah and Torro supermarkets, Basismarkt dry groceries stores, Boekanier discount liquor stores, Verduyn and P. Van Dijken supermarkets and hypermarkets, and Konmar hypermarkets. The performance of this division was judged to be satisfactory during 1980-1982. Although each enterprise varied in size and operating approach, the group as a whole was able to withstand the intensified competition in Dutch food retailing and showed substantial growth during this period.

Mail Order Division

The division came into existence in 1980 as a result of many acquisitions of Dutch and foreign mail-order organizations. The components include Keurkoop, Concordia Mail (Belgium), Interselection (France), Kurfurst Warenversand (West Germany, Austria, and Switzerland), Lekturama mail-order publishers, and Nederlands Talen Instituut, which offers correspondence courses.

Financial Services Division

The division is comprised of Staal Bankiers, Vendopolis insurance agencies, and Voorschotbank Rotterdamse Credietbank. Because of the tight money market situation and a prolonged recession in the housing and durable goods sector, the division has experienced limited growth.

Services Division

A cross-section of diverse service enterprises constitutes this division: Evro temporary employment services, Cemsto office cleaning services, Tecso public transportation cleaning and finishing services, hospital services, moving and distribution services, maintenance services, laundries, roller towels and soap dispenser services, and security services, among others. The division also offers several miscellaneous services, such as a hostess training institute, City Courier (express delivery of small packages), wholesale trading in advanced electronic consumer goods, cable television, tax-free sales outside the EEC, Intervendex (international merchandising in foreign countries), and Vendopack International Supply Service.

Many components of the group's hard goods and services division were added during 1978 and 1979 when the group made the strategic decision to achieve growth through the route of specialty retail shops rather than emphasizing traditional low-margin department stores and food business.

International Division

The group has been pursuing a strong international strategy through direct ownership, as well as participation in the United States, Japan, and Brazil. The goals of the International Division have been spelled out as "diversification of interests in countries with good growth prospects and favorable attitudes toward business in general."[8] The United States has continued to remain the primary focus of international programs, where the group has been active since 1979, when foreign direct investments were made in the Outlet Company, Dillard's department stores, H. J. Wilson Co. (catalog showroom chain), and Cole Corporation. The group also established a subsidiary, Vendamerica Inc., in Greenwich, Connecticut, in 1980 with a twofold objective of providing information on retailing developments in the United States and developing synergistic relationships between the group's U.S. companies and its activities in Europe, Japan, and Brazil.

The Outlet Company. The Outlet Company, based in Providence, Rhode Island, was the group's first target in the United States. The company owned a chain of stores in the East and a string of radio and television stations at the time of investment. The profile of this organization underwent a significant metamorphosis in 1980 when its various retail divisions were sold out, and it announced an agreement for its merger into Columbia Pictures Industries. Before this merger went through, however, Columbia itself agreed to be acquired by Coca-Cola Company in a major diversification move. Thus, the Outlet Company is now a part of the Coca-Cola organization, and Vroom & Dreesman continues to maintain its holdings in the form of a convertible preferred issue.

Dillard's. Dillard's is one of the leading chains of department stores in the United States, headquartered in Little Rock, Arkansas. The company operates 56 stores in eight southwestern states with a total area of 7,150,000 square feet. It is believed to be one of the fastest-growing department store chains in the country, reflected by the following financial indicators:

Year Ended Jan. 31	Sales (millions)	Net Income (millions)
1980	391	8.3
1981	470	8.5
1982	592	16.25

H. J. Wilson Co. The group's holdings in this Louisiana-based catalog merchandise chain is 21.3 percent of the shares outstanding. Wilson, like Dillard's, is one of Vroom & Dreesmann's prized investments. It has seventy showrooms in 11 states, recording sales and earnings for the 1981 fiscal year at $403 million and $12.7 million, respectively, compared to $297.8 million and $11 million, respectively, for fiscal year 1980.[9]

Cole National Corporation. A Cleveland-based chain of small specialty kiosks, Cole represents the fourth stake of the group in the United States with a participation of 14.5 percent. This is a unique operation of more than 1,500 shops, organized in five divisions: optical, gift stores operating as Things Remembered, craft stores under the name the Craft Showcase, key shops, and cookie shops called the Original Cookie Company. Many of the optical departments and key kiosks are operated by Cole Corporation as leased departments in national chains, such as Sears, Penney's, and Montgomery Ward.

In August 1980, Cole purchased 41.5 percent of Child-World, the second largest toy retailer in the United States, with 68 stores in 15 states.

Through minority participation in some of the leading retail chains in the United States, Vroom & Dreesmann has deliberately kept a low profile in the management of these companies. It has preferred to remain a silent partner in these fast-growing organizations, showing great confidence in the capabilities of the present management. During 1980-1981, the group had reached, in principle, an agreement with W. R. Grace & Co. to acquire a 50 percent interest in its retailing operations, but the deal apparently fell through when it was announced in November 1981 that the two companies had ended their talks.

The group's international diversification strategy was reinforced when it extended its operations to Japan by acquiring 3 percent participation in UNY Co. Ltd., one of the leading retail companies in Japan, in October 1980. UNY operates 98 superstores, ten drugstores under the name Hearts, My Travel travel agencies, Circle K convenience stores, Winchell doughnut shops, and Albu telephone sales service, selling food products directly to consumers. In addition, UNY has four subsidiaries: a specialty chain of 122 stores selling traditional Japanese clothing such as kimonos, a smaller chain of eight mini-superstores, a housing company engaged in building and selling residential housing, and a fifty-fifty joint venture in real estate with Toyota Motor Company. UNY has also joined Comp-U-Card Company of the United States to pioneer nonstore retailing in Japan.

In Brazil, the group's interests consist of total ownership of Ultralar, a 46-store chain selling household goods, furniture and consumer electronics, and 50 percent participation in Ultracred, a consumer credit company with 44 branch offices located in five states in midsouthern Brazil.

In Europe, the group owns 100 percent interest in Hunkemoller Belgium, a fast-growing specialty chain selling foundation garments, underwear, and swimwear, an extension of Hunkemoller's domestic operations. The group also has a minority interest in Cody, a middle-sized food discount chain with sixty sales points in southwest Belgium.

AHOLD N.V.

Ahold was founded in 1887 as a 120 square foot neighborhood grocery store in Oostzaan, Holland. In 1900, the owners moved the company to Zaandam, where, over time, they built a central warehouse, a confectionery plant, and a baking unit and operated 54 grocery stores by 1917. The company grew steadily in the next thirty years, adding 198 stores, a larger bakery, a coffee-roasting and tea-packaging plant, a restaurant, and a small Amsterdam dairy. The company was converted into a public limited company in 1948, and the early 1950s witnessed its adoption of two critical retailing innovations: its first self-service store in 1952 and the first supermarket in 1955. Since then, the organization has grown in various directions, maintaining its stronghold in the field of food retailing. In October 1976, it moved into international retailing by opening its first supermarket in Spain; the following year, it entered the U.S. retail food market by acquiring the Bi-Lo chain of 98 supermarkets. Ahold is believed to be a traditional and conservative company relative to its competitors in the Netherlands. Its main business activities are divided into three groups:

1. Retail trade in the Netherlands: Consists of Albert Heijn and Simon supermarkets and self-service stores, Miro hypermarkets, Alberto wine and liquor discount stores, Etos discount drugstore, Nettomarkt self-service department store, Toko campsite stores, distribution centers, and central meat processing plants.

2. Restaurants—Institutional and Recreational Activities: Includes AC restaurants in the Netherlands, Belgium, and West Germany, Albert Jeijn Grootverbruik (institutional sales), APCO catering services, and Ostara vacation centers.

3. Ahold Food Production: Comprises a bread section, a pastry bakery, meat products, milk and dairy products, a wine bottler, and production and packaging of coffee and tea, chocolate, and other dry groceries.

Ahold Espana

Ahold's international operations started in 1976 when it opened its first supermarket overseas in Spain under the name CadaDia. The 1979 municipal elections paved the way for obtaining building and operating licenses. Ahold built a 55,500 square foot distribution center with office facilities in Villalba to provide operational support to 24 stores the company had planned to build by 1980. Ahold had also diversified its activities in Spain by buying a majority interest in a highly profitable sherry house (*bodega*). The business performance of all types of stores in Spain looked very promising, with sales and profit figures continuing to rise significantly. But the year 1981 did not prove as encouraging; sales began to decline as a result of economic recession and rising unemployment. In this year, three *superdescuentos* (small-size discount stores) were added. Due to bureaucratic delays in the issuance of permits, no new *supermercados* were opened in 1981. Thus, Ahold Espana operated 18 *supermercados* and 11 *superdescuentos* by the end of 1981.

Bi-Lo

Bi-Lo supermarket chain was Ahold's first venture in the United States. This Maudlin, South Carolina-based regional supermarket chain was acquired in 1977 and proved to be a significant addition for the organization. The chain's financial performance has continued to improve despite the recessionary trends and competition that had dominated the U.S. retail industry until 1982. The new management gradually introduced a selected assortment of beer and wine in Bi-Lo supermarkets and also introduced changes in the system of purchasing and processing meat. The number of outlets rose from 110 in 1979 to 129 in 1981, and the corresponding sales figures rose from $547.4 million to $728 million.

Giant Food Stores

The strategy of international expansion continued in 1981 when Ahold acquired Giant Food Stores, a Carlisle, Pennsylvania, supermarket chain, which operates 31 supermarkets mainly in Pennsylvania. The 1981 performance of Giant Food Stores was regarded as satisfactory, with a sales volume of $44 million for the 1 ½ month period during which the ownership rested with Ahold. The new management has plans to expand its operations and increase gradually the number of stores in the 1980s.

KONINKLIJKE BIJENKORF BEHEER (KBB)

The origin of this large retailing group in the Netherlands can be traced back to 1870 when a modest store, selling thread, ribbon, and drapery items, was set up under the name Magazijn de Bijenkorf. This was the time when the world's first department store "Au Bon Marche" had started its operations in Paris. One could hardly imagine that De Bijenkorf was the nucleus of a gigantic retail enterprise complex in the Netherlands that proliferated soon in The Hague, Rotterdam, Eindhoven, and Arnhem.

Today KBB is one of the leading trading groups with diverse retailing institutions and services. De Bijenkorf stores were later joined by Hema, a mass merchandise chain of variety stores founded in 1926 along the line of British Woolworth. Hema stores are located in practically every Dutch town and account for the highest volume of sales and personnel in the KBB family. The 1970s witnessed a major diversification in this group in the form of new retailing formulas designed to serve changing consumer lifestyles. KBB responded to these developments by establishing Maxis/ Trefcenter superstores, Praxis do-it-yourself centers, Mobell warehouse showrooms, and specialized sport stores under the name Perry Sport. It also made its debut in purely service projects such as Robex winter sports centers and Kilimpex Total Care Centers for cleaning office buildings. These centers were set up in collaboration with other companies as joint ventures.

KBB has also moved beyond national borders. It entered into a joint venture with a Swiss financial institution to bring into existence KBB SA Geneva. It was this financing subsidiary that broke new ground in the international sector: KBB Far East Trading Ltd. in Hong Kong and KBB Holding Company U.S.A. In 1980 the latter took over a 100-store chain of variety stores, Macks, considered to be compatible with Hema in terms of assortment of merchandise, size, and location. This linkage between Hema and Macks was considered significant from the viewpoint of possible gains to both sides through managerial synergy and exchange of know-how. Macks Stores Inc. is based in Sanford, North Carolina, and its stores are spread over North and South Carolina, Georgia, and Virginia. A brief description of KBB's major retail businesses is presented below.[10]

De Bijenkorf

These are the monumental department stores that laid the foundation of KBB as a leading retail company in the Netherlands. Located in five key cities, the stores focus on fashion, interior furnishings, gifts, and recreation products. In response to changing consumer profiles and problems created by growing urbanization, more emphasis is being placed on fashion, home furnishings, modern living styles, and parking garages. The old establishments, such as the one in Amsterdam, are being expanded and reconstructed to provide an ambience that reflects today's consumers.

Hema

A comparatively smaller store with an average of 17,000 items compared to 250,000 in De Bijenkorf, Hema has 72 wholly owned and 102 franchised stores spread over the country, even in small provincial towns with 10,000 inhabitants. A typical Hema store carries 30 percent textiles, 30 percent grocery, and 40 percent other nongrocery items. The chain determines its own quality standards and undertakes commodity tests to determine whether manufacturers' product offerings conform to these standards. With few exceptions, Hema sells under its own label and does not carry manufacturers' brands. The sales system used in a Hema store is a mix of personal service, semiservice, and self-service, depending on the nature of the department.

Maxis/Trefcenter

These are superstores or hypermarkets with a complete package of consumer goods—durable, nondurable, and grocery—offered under one roof. A typical Maxis store is located on the outskirts of a large city as a free-standing store with about 40,000 articles. Each usually contains a self-service restaurant and a few leased small shops.

Trefcenters are usually smaller and located in a town, as part of a shopping center, often with other stores, offices, and recreation centers. A distinctive feature of these stores is that they carry the best-known brands (unlike house brands in the case of Hema) at a price considerably lower than those set or suggested by suppliers and manufacturers.

Praxis

KBB's response to burgeoning building and repair costs and customers' needs for do-it-yourself came in the form of Praxis, a chain of stores selling a variety of building materials normally bought by household customers to do the jobs themselves. The articles sold carry full information to enable the customers to make correct choices from a wide and detailed assortment. Run mostly on a self-service basis, a typical Praxis store carries 10,000 low-priced articles displayed on about 3,000 square meters of floor area.

Perry Sport

KBB has met the rising interest in leisure and recreation activity. By setting up the Perry Sport chain, the company created a specialized outlet for the sale of sport and recreation articles used in swimming, tennis, skiing, running, and camping. A typical Perry Sport store sells some 8,000 articles, mostly on a self-service basis, with attractive bargains.

THE BRENNINKMEYERS

The Brenninkmeyers family has a long history in retailing. It started selling in the Netherlands in 1841 and gradually built up a mercantile empire in Europe, spread over the Netherlands, West Germany, England, Belgium, and Switzerland. In 1965, it acquired the 12-unit specialty chain Ohrbach's which it operates through its U.S. holding company, Amcena Corporation. In 1977, it moved to Brazil. Top management is believed to be well paid and ranked at a high level by industry for discipline and ability to merchandise quality soft goods at low prices. The Brenninkmeyers is considered to be a close-mouthed and highly centralized organization. Its retailing activities are controlled by Unicena, the holding company that looks after its retailing and investment interests over the world.

In 1976-1977, Brenninkmeyers operated fifty stores in the Netherlands with an estimated sales of $250 million. It also operated one hundred stores in Germany and 71 stores in Britain, with sales of $1.5 billion and $500 million, respectively. In France, it opened its first store in 1971, but observers say it misjudged the fashion habits of French women who were more accustomed to boutique shopping.[11] The company operated these stores under different names, such as C&A Modes, Brenninkmeyers, P. J. Voss, and Mateor.

Similarly in the United States, some C&A executives thought that they failed to upgrade their merchandise to match American tastes. The company operated a store in Brooklyn, New York, for a number of years under the name C&A Modes but was not able to obtain a permanent foothold in the New York market. The acquisition of Ohrbach's was followed by that of Maurice, an apparel retailer in the Midwest, in 1978. The negotiations for taking over Miller-Wohl, a New Jersey-based women's apparel chain, had reached a fairly conclusive point, but it is believed they fell through.[12]

DELHAIZE LE LION

Established in 1867 in Brussels, Delhaize Le Lion is the second largest Belgian retailing company, operating 97 Delhaize supermarkets and forty stores offering a limited grocery assortment under the name Dial.[13] The company also operates eight Super Beauty Centers and 41 gas stations. The domestic retailing activity is supported by three distribution centers and 385 vehicles, especially equipped to carry different types of merchandise. The 1981 sales of Delhaize operations amounted to BF 43.28 billion, or approximately $1 billion.

Initially the company was heavily involved in manufacturing operations, but in 1945 it decided to close down all of them except the coffee-roasting division and wine bottling warehouse, which have continued to remain profitable.

Delhaize's international operations are currently limited to the United States and controlled by Delhaize Le Lion America, Inc., a holding company incorporated in the United States. This company has made equity investments in two U.S. retailing companies, Food Giant, Inc. (100 percent) and Food Town Stores, Inc. (15.4 percent). It has also advanced loans totaling $19.7 million to Food Giant, Inc.

Food Giant, Inc. (formerly Alterman Foods) operates a chain of 89 supermarkets in Georgia and Alabama. Fifty-four of these stores and a distribution center are located in the Atlanta region. Food Giant is involved in the wholesale business, supplying fresh food and groceries to independent stores. The company suffered a loss of $2.84 million in 1982, partly due to unfavorable environmental factors facing the retail industry as a whole and partly because of poor organizational strategies. Significant changes were planned for 1982 in several areas, such as structure, store layout, and warehouse allocations.[14]

Food Town Stores, on the other hand, showed an excellent financial performance during 1980 and 1981, with an increase in net income from $15.28 million to $19.31 million. The company operated 141 supermarkets, mainly in Virginia and North and South Carolina, with the support of two distribution centers, located in Salisbury, North Carolina, with a total floor space of 928,565 square feet. A new warehouse was also expected to be ready in 1983. Food Town sales registered a 22.6 percent increase in 1981, mainly as a result of the opening of 37 new supermarkets. The company planned to expand its market coverage by adding new stores.

DOCKS DE FRANCE

Docks De France is the fourth largest retail company in France, operating 35 hypermarkets under the name Mammouth and 157 super-markets, including 19 in Spain. The French outlets include Nova and Suma supermarkets. Like other European companies, Docks De France has food processing, meat processing, and baking facilities to support its retail operations.

The U.S. operation of this company, Lil' Champ, is a chain of 162 convenience drive-in stores of the 7-11 type, accounting for sales of $49 million.[15] The stores are located in northeast and central Florida and sell mainly groceries, dairy products, health and beauty aids, beer and wine, soft drinks, snack foods, tobacco products, paperback books, and magazines. In addition, 66 units are equipped with facilities for the sale of gasoline, of which 33 are company owned.

PROMODES

Promodes is the third largest distribution company in France engaged in a variety of wholesaling and retailing activities in the domestic market as well as overseas. It was established as a food distributor in 1961 through a merger of several regional and family-owned food wholesalers. The company accounted for a net sales of 15 billion francs and provided employment to over 19,000 persons in 1981.[16]

Its wholesale operations consist of the Promogros franchise network and Promocash and Multi-cash cash-and-carry self-service wholesaling centers. The franchise network offers management know-how and a wide range of technical services to retail stores of all sizes. These operations have also been developed in the Madrid area in Spain.

In the retailing field, the Promodes Group operates over 1,000 outlets under the name Champion. These include neighborhood and self-service stores, as well as discount supermarkets. In the Madrid area, eighty limited-assortment discount stores are managed under the name DIA. In addition, the company is one of the leading owners of hypermarkets in France. It operates 23 hypermarkets in France, known as Continent, with a total area of 3,903,021 square feet. Through subsidiaries, five hypermarkets are operated in Spain, and another five are operated on a franchise basis in West Germany.

The company operates a number of production and packaging plants and full-line regional distribution centers to support its trading operations. It also runs a chain of 13 cafeterias in various shopping centers in France under the name Presto.

In February 1980, Promodes moved to the United States and acquired 100 percent ownership of Red Food Stores, a chain of forty grocery stores located in Tennessee and north Georgia. The chain's annual sales amounted to $305 million in 1980.

AGACHE-WILLOT

Agache-Willot S.A. is a holding company that came into existence after the merger of M. et J. Willot & Cie with Etablissements Agache, a major public textile company, in 1967.

M. et J. Willot & Cie (M. J. Willot Company) was a family business conducted by the Willot brothers—Jean-Pierre, Bernard, Antoine, and Regis—founded by their grandfather to make surgical bandages. The brothers began to think beyond bandages and started buying a number of unsuccessful textile mills in Lille, their home town, about 145 miles from Paris.

With the acquisition of the Agache textile operations in the late 1950s, the family business went outside Lille, under the name Agache-Willot, with its retailing headquarters in Paris and its textile offices in Lille. Starting in 1969, Agache-Willot made a number of important acquisitions in the retailing field: Belle Jardinière department stores in 1969, Au Bon Marché in 1970, the Ted Lapidus group of fashion boutiques, the Conforama home furnishing chain in 1976, and a Belgian department store, Galeries Anspach, in 1978. It also acquired Saint Frères textile products company in 1969 and the Boussac complex of textile and apparel manufacturing business in 1978. These acquisitions turned Agache-Willot into one of the leading family business houses in France and generated both resources and confidence, particularly because the financial performance of most of the retailing companies improved significantly after acquisition. Corporate sales in 1979 were nearly $3 billion. In 1979, Agache-Willot bought the Korvettes discount chain for $55 million from Arlen Realty and Development Company, New York.[17]

At the time of acquisition, Korvettes comprised fifty stores, thirty located in the New York metropolitan area. Korvettes began operation in the United States in 1948 as discounters of hard goods, brand name appliances, tools, and luggage. It adhered to the business philosophy of keeping overhead down and stock-turn up, resulting in intensive growth. New stores were added, with the heaviest concentration in the tri-state area of New York, New Jersey, and Connecticut. Before being acquired by Agache-Willot in 1979, Korvettes ownership had changed hands twice, once in 1966 when it was merged with Spartan Industry, a manufacturer of soft goods with several small retail outlets, and later in 1977 when Arlen Realty and Development Corporation, the nation's largest publicly held real estate company, merged with Spartan Industry in 1977. The real estate recession of the mid 1970s severely affected Arlen's financial position, saddled with a debt of $1.3 billion. Korvettes' management in 1977 decided to reposition the stores in the high fashion apparel market and to that end allocated funds to upgrade the store facilities and project an image of quality. The strategy, however, did not work as expected.

The company's financial picture continued to remain bleak. In 1978, preceding the takover, it suffered a loss of $110.9 million on an estimated sales of $600 million.[18] Agache-Willot found it extremely difficult to pilot the sinking Korvettes, let alone turn it around. Within two years of the takeover, it decided to withdraw. Its acquisitions in France had not been doing well either. Boussac-Saint Frères suffered acute financial problems, so much so that to keep it going, Agache-Willot was forced to sell some prime possessions, including Au Bon Marché and Conforama.[19]

HABITAT MOTHERCARE

Habitat Mothercare is the name that Habitat, a London-based retail chain, adopted after its merger with Mothercare Company, another British chain selling maternity and children's goods, in January, 1982. Both companies entered the U.S. retailing scene before merger.

Mothercare acquired the 112-store DeKon corporation in April 1976 which retailed similar product lines. The chain of stores acquired was

Mother-To-Be, a name retained for one group of stores. Subsequently, the company set up new stores under its own name, with its first store established in 1977. Today, the chain has over 200 outlets carrying three different names: Mother-To-Be, Mothercare, and Maternity Modes.

Habitat entered the United States in 1977, but not through acquistion. Instead it established Conran's, at Citicorp Center, in New York City, a 40,000 square foot store. By July 1980, it had set up another five in New Jersey, Washington, D.C., Manhasset, Long Island, Fairfax Country, Virginia, and Philadelphia.

Both the companies, now merged into Habitat Mothercare, are mature organizations with a tremendous reputation for creativity, quality, and service. The first Mothercare store opened in the United Kingdom in 1961 under the leadership of Selim K. Zilkha, a U.S. citizen who bought the franchise rights from Prenatal, a well-known French chain, and applied them to the chain of maternity shops he took over. The new company was given the name Mothercare; by 1982, there were over 200 shops in the United Kingdom and over 400 throughout the world. Mothercare subsidiaries today operate in Austria, Belgium, Denmark, the Netherlands, Norway, Sweden, Switzerland, Germany, Canada, and New Zealand, in addition to the United States. In Europe, the company is also engaged in mail-order business in its primary product lines. Zilkha stayed with the company until 1982.

The foundation of Habitat was laid by Terence O. Conran, who believed that customers should not be given a furnishing design. They should participate in selecting and arranging the merchandise for their homes rather than following the suggestions of retailers. A typical Conran's store, based on this philosophy, presents a variety of life-style choices with a merchandise mix far broader than that normally found in American home furnishing stores. Conran's market is predominantly middle-class young people furnishing for the first time. It has also been trying to catch them when they move into subsequent life cycles and need to furnish their homes again. "Habitat is not some quirky organization producing only things for a minority," Terence Conran once said, "We design and produce serious, down-to-earth, sensible products."[20] Conran's had established 52 stores by 1981. The merged parent, Habitat Mothercare, reported in its 1983 annual report its total world turnover of £309.7 million and total trading profit of £27.4 million, as against £255 million and £20.6 million, respectively, reported in 1982. The number of Conran's and Mothercare retail stores increased from 481 in 1982 to 506 in 1983. The company's design subsidiaries based in the United Kingdom, France, and the United States are involved in design consulting and provide major support to its retail activities.

Habitat in March 1982 signed an agreement to open Habitat shops in Japan in partnership with the Seibu Department Store. By March 1983, the joint venture resulted in six stores in Japan, with three more scheduled to open the same year.

B.A.T. INDUSTRIES PLC

B.A.T. Industries Ltd., with headquarters in London, is Britain's third largest business enterprise. Its principal activity is the worldwide manufacture of tobacco products. It also has considerable international interests in retailing, paper, packaging and printing, cosmetics, and other activities. The B.A.T. Group employs about 2.8 million people in subsidiaries located in 77 countries on six continents. It is organized through seven operating groups: British American Tobacco Co., B.A.T. Store Holdings, the Wiggins Teape Group, Mardon Packaging International, British American Cosmetics, Interversa GmbH, and Batus Inc. It also holds a 49.9 percent share in Horten A. G., a West Germany retail store.

B.A.T. Industries' foreign direct investment in U.S. retailing has been on a much larger scale compared to other European investors through its U.S. subsidiary, Brown & Williamson Tobacco, based in Kentucky.

Brown & Williamson's first major investment in U.S. retailing dates back to 1972 when it acquired an 80 percent interest in Kohl Corporation, a Wisconsin-based grocery and department store chain. The second round of investment occurred in 1973 when Brown & Williamson acquired 100 percent ownership of Gimbels Bros. and Saks Fifth Avenue, two prestigious retail establishments in New York, for about $210 million. In 1979, the parent company announced plans to establish a new retail group within the corporate office to take care of these three acquisitions. Later in 1980, the diversified U.S. operations of B.A.T. Industries were brought under the single umbrella of Batus, Inc., which was formed as a new holding and management center for the combined tobacco, retail, and paper interests.

Today Batus Inc. is one of the top one hundred industrial corporations with consolidated sales of $4.6 billion and an operating income of $419 million in 1981. The retail division Batus achieved sales of over $2 billion and an operating income of $127 million in this year.[21] In March 1982 it announced the signing of a merger agreement providing for the acquisition of Marshall Field, Chicago. This was the third round of acquisition made by the British holding company in retailing industry within a period of ten years. Batus Inc. was welcomed by the management of Marshall Field because of an unfriendly bid made by a group of investors headed by Carl Icahn to acquire a 30 percent stake in the stock of Marshall Field.[22]

CONCLUSION

The profiles of major European investors presented in this chapter show that regardless of the degree of success they have attained in the U.S.

market, most had accumulated considerable experience and generated enough surplus capital before making a stake in U.S. retailing. They had gained an in-depth understanding of a cross-section of retailing operations not only in their respective homelands but in foreign countries as well. They did not take the U.S. market for granted. On the other hand, they had shown their keen desire to make the best of their U.S. investment and to that end most outlined serious plans and programs to develop and expand the retail enterprises they had acquired.

Some investors, however, seemed to have had little experience in retailing. Their goal was to make a sound investment in areas that were not saturated. Examples are Générale Occidentale, a holding company based in Paris, which acquired Grand Union; Franz Haniel & Cie, a West German shipping company, which acquired the Scrivner chain of food and department stores; Sears Holding, a London-based holding company, which acquired a number of specialty chains; and Heinrich Bauer Verlag, a German magazine publisher, which acquired a variety store chain, Winn's.

APPENDIX: OUR BELGIAN FRIENDS*

When Delhaize purchased a block of Food Town stock in 1974, it became the grocery company's largest stockholder. The sale was mutually advantageous. For Delhaize, it meant the investment in an innovative and profitable company in the United States. For Food Town shareholders, it means an opportunity to cash in on profits derived from as much as 17 years of holding Food Town stock.

The Delhaize story is also a notable one. It was July 1867 when two Belgian brothers, Jules and Auguste Delhaize, opened several small food stores and a supply business for other independent stores. These one-time teachers of high school economics called the new business, appropriately enough, Delhaize Brothers and were later joined by other brothers and their brother-in-law in their venture.

The Delhaizes proved to be innovative businessmen and soon opened other stores. At the time, all grocery items were subject to constant bargaining at the retail level, but Delhaize realized that just wouldn't do. Instead, Delhaize Brothers was among the first companies to sell at a fixed retail price in Europe. They also set a first in organizing as a chain of stores rather than a single outlet. Several years later in 1883, Delhaize built its first warehouse in suburban Brussels, Belgium and began operation of food product manufacturing facilities.

In spite of two world wars, Delhaize continued its strong growth, but in 1945, it elected to close all of its manufacturing plants except the Coffee Roasting Division and wine bottling warehouse. Both remain open today as

---

*Reproduced by permission from *The Profile*, bulletin published by Food Town, Twenty-Fifth Anniversary issue, vol. 10, no. 11, December 1982.

profitable and reputable contributions to the total Delhaize company.

Over the years, Delhaize has experienced many important achievements. In 1950, it had grown to operate nearly 400 small food stores and provide wholesale services to a total of 1,667 food outlets. In 1957, the first full-fledged supermarket became a reality, and its Fresh Products Distribution Center opened in 1963. It was among the first in Europe. A year earlier, Delhaize moved from a family owned operation to a publicly held company.

But it was in 1974 that Delhaize sought interest in companies in the United States. Growth in Belgium was proving more and more difficult due to an environment full of restrictions. Before opening each store, for example, every Belgian operation must seek authorization from several departments of the State government. The size of each store must correspond to State regulations. Also, the State decides for the store what hour it can open and does not allow any store to remain open after 8:00 P.M. Most important and restricting, the State controls gross margins of the retail trade and consequently maintains a level of prices which protects stores with poor efficiency. If a company sells any item for any reason below cost, the State prosecutes. Competition is restricted at all times. In a population of 10 million people and 20,000 stores, 45% of the retail trade volume is accounted for by 2% of the stores because of limitations by the government.

Realizing that retailing had become more difficult in Europe and particularly in Belgium, Delhaize management began investigating ways to expand their company. Among those ideas tossed about were placing its resources into the development of fast food operations or perhaps a reentry into the manufacturing of some types of food product manufacturing. But the more logical and appropriate answer seemed to be to remain in a field that was most familiar to the company and to simply seek interests outside of Europe. It was at this point that research was begun in the United States for possible investment in supermarket operations located here.

After visiting the United States many times, it became clear that Delhaize and Food Town were meant for each other. The location in the Southeast was a growing market. Food Town was exceptionally well managed by a team to which Delhaize felt an immediate attraction. Food Town management had been successful in creating an excellent spirit in their company which was particualarly evident even to Europeans unfamiliar with the ways of Americans.

Delhaize says that because the Food Town operating philosophy is so different from other companies, it has learned from Food Town. Though many of the techniques are difficult to apply in the old continent because of differences in governments and lifestyles, the knowledge is certain to help in Delhaize's continued interest in the United States marketplace.

Delhaize Le Lion's sales in 1981 were approximately one billion U.S. dollars. At the end of last year, it operated 97 Belgian supermarkets, eight beauty centers, 41 gas stations, 40 stores offering a limited grocery assortment, and supplied 125 other affiliated stores. Coupled with its U.S. grocery holdings the totals are even larger.

Food Town's newer stores, as well as their advertising, now highlights the Delhaize logotype lion. The new logo is a gentle reminder of the continued interest shown in Food Town by our Belgian friends.

NOTES

1. "A & P: Should You Invest along with the Germans?" *Financial World*, February 15, 1979, pp. 16-20.

2. "A Bit of Tengel," *Economist,* April 19, 1980, p. 66.

3. "Europe Still Eyes the U.S.," *Supermarket News*, June 14, 1982, p. 10.

4. "What Will Tomorrow's Customers Want" (Karlsruhe: Mann GmbH, 1978), p. 21.

5. *Wall Street Journal*, April 29, 1981, p. 48.

6. "Vroom, Vroom," *Economist*, January 12, 1980, p. 74.

7. Vroom & Dreesmann, *Annual Report, 1980-1981* and *1981-1982.*

8. Ibid., *1981-1982*, p. 20.

9. Based on data published in ibid. for 1980-1981 and 1981-1982.

10. The following descriptions are based on information published in a company brochure, "KBB in Outline" (Amsterdam, 1981).

11. "A Revived Miller-Wohl Lures a Dutch Bidder," *Business Week,* September 5, 1977, p. 34.

12. Ibid., p. 36.

13. Delhaize Freres & Cie "Le Lion" s.a., *Annual Report, 1981.*

14. Ibid., p. 15.

15. Lil' Champ, *Annual Report, 1982*, p. 2.

16. Promodes, *Rapport Annuel, 1981.*

17. See Isadore Barmash, *More Than They Bargained For: The Rise and Fall of Korvettes* (New York: Lebhar-Friedman Books, 1981), pp. 247-48.

18. Ibid., p. 237.

19. "Brothers Who Want Korvettes," *New York Times*, February 4, 1979, sec. 3, p. 7-1.

20. Eric Clark, "Conran's Dual Challenge," *Marketing*, August 5, 1982, p. 19.

21. Batus, *1981 Annual Report,* pp. 1-17.

22. Allan J. Wax, "White Knights Grow Scarce," *Newsday,* April 17, 1983, p. 84.

5

Motivations of European Investors

The profiles of major European companies that have made large investments in the United States reflect a gradual sophistication and maturity on the part of European retailing. Why are these and many other European business houses looking to U.S. retail companies? Why was there a spate of direct investment from Europe in U.S. retailing during the 1970s? Why did retailing generate so much inflow of foreign capital in the 1970s? What is the real goal of European investors: a safe investment, a second home, a learning experience, or a strategic move to exploit new opportunities? These questions need to be resolved.

ENVIRONMENTAL OR MACROLEVEL FACTORS

A variety of environmental or macrolevel factors are believed to have played an instrumental role in attracting European companies. These factors encompassed both the U.S. and European environment.

U.S. Environment

It is widely accepted that the trend of European investments picked up in the early 1970s as a result of the dollar devaluation that occurred between August 1971 and July 1973. The U.S. dollar registered a significant decline relative to other currencies between 1971 and 1977. It fell 32 percent relative to the German mark, 44 percent relative to the Swiss franc, 27 percent relative to the Dutch guilder, and 32 percent relative to the Japanese yen. This led to sharp drops in the value of U.S. stocks, particularly during 1969-1970 and again during 1973-1974. The steady decline in the value of most stocks was viewed as a special opportunity by many European companies, especially British companies, which tended to assign higher price-earning multiples to retail stocks.

The result was that many U.S. companies could get a better sale price for their stock from foreign investors—in some cases as much as ten times the average earnings, compared to seven or eight times the earnings offered by domestic investors.

The change in the relative values of various currencies had an impact on comparative cost schedules. The differentials of manufacturing costs such as raw material, labor, and power changed significantly, so much so that investment in United State enterprises became more attractive, especially in the wake of a strong United States economy. The unit labor costs in the United States registered a lower increase than in many European countries, Canada, and Japan, For example,

Citibank recently analyzed the growth in hourly wage rates among manufacturing workers between 1970 and 1977. The analysis found that the U.S. has experienced the lowest percentage increase in manufacturing wages—11 percent over the 9 years period. The study included eleven other industrialized countries from Europe and Japan. Rates rose over the nine years 30 percent in Canada, 33 percent in Britain, 54 percent in the Netherlands, 63 percent in West Germany and 77 percent in Italy. (The wages were measured in local currencies and adjusted for inflation.) In terms of dollar wage per hour, the U.S. had the highest average wage in 1970, but the seventh highest in 1979.[1]

U.S. retail companies comprise several organizational types: independent unit stores (privately run small grocery and specialty shops) and newer institutions such as department stores, supermarkets, and discounters, which normally functioned as a chain of several stores, with a network of other facilities, such as processing plants, warehouses, and administrative offices. This meant a considerable investment in real estate for the average retail company. The market value of this real estate itself was of the order of several hundred thousand dollars in many companies, more so for companies located in the sunbelt states. The post-1973 period was noted for an unprecedented appreciation in the value of real estate, an added attraction to investors in retailing. The French owners of Korvettes, thus, were keen to buy the Korvettes store properties owned by Arlen and leased to Korvettes. The French prefer to own the real estate in which they function.[2]

The United States offered a vast and relatively homogeneous domestic market, with a compatible sociocultural fabric and similar business practices and systems. The country has a sizable concentration of various ethnic groups originating in Europe and with similar religious backgrounds. The cosmopolitan character of U.S. culture, the broad outlook of various trading communities, and the balanced view taken by the U.S. press would also be regarded as factors conducive to foreign investors' decision.

The U.S. economy was considered stable and prosperous, not as affected by political turbulence and public policy in relation to business as were many European economies. Public policy in the United States was relatively more pro-big business and less detrimental to the expansion and growth of large business organizations as long as it did not lead to a serious concentration of economic power. The U.S. retail industry crossed the trillion-dollar mark in 1981 in spite of inflation and unemployment.

Hands-Off Policy of the U.S. Government

U.S. antitrust laws and related rules and procedures were designed primarily for domestic business and did not come in the way of foreign investors as long as they remained outside such critical areas as defense and banking. In fact, foreign investors are exempt from certain obligations of domestic businesses. They do not have to pay capital gains tax on real estate sales or meet the margin requirements of 50 percent on the purchase price of stock. One strong contributory factor in the direct investment trend was the lesser vulnerability of mergers-acquisitions involving foreign companies to the antitrust laws. U.S. fiscal policy does not discriminate between foreign and domestic investors. The process of structuring and implementing foreign acquisition is not affected by special tax obstacles. Rarely was a proposal of foreign acquisition of a U.S. retail business rejected except when it caused a serious imbalance in the prevailing competitive structure. One of the reasons explaining U.S. companies' preference for being acquired by foreign companies was the relative ease with which proposals from the latter were approved, bypassing certain regulatory checks normally applicable to domestic acquisitions.

The benign legal environment proved as helpful in entering into and expanding within the United States market as in phasing out or quitting, as seen in the case of French owners of Korvettes. To the new owners of A&P, Fed Mart, and several others, it was easier or much less cumbersome to effect layoffs, dismiss employees on short notice, or close down stores at selected locations any time management decided than what it would have been in their respective home countries.[3]

European Environment

Public policy in most European countries was not entirely in favor of the growth and expansion of medium and large-sized retail companies during the late sixties and early seventies. The homeland of most European retail companies presented a legal environment especially detrimental to the growth of many leading industrial enterprises, both manufacturing and trading. Such enterprises had to encounter a variety of barriers, such as discriminatory treatment meted out to retail companies in the United Kingdom in the matter of investment grants, depreciation and other allowances, stiffer planning and zoning regulations in Belgium, the Netherlands, and West Germany, and so on. The main purpose of such regulations is to protect small retailers, to maintain a balance between commercial and noncommercial activities, and to protect residential areas from the hazards of business expansion.

The economic situation in Europe had started to deteriorate during the 1973 oil crisis and the ensuing inflation. The EEC held out promise to its members and was instrumental in strengthening the economy of member countries during the sixties and early seventies; however, inflation and unemployment plagued these economies seriously in the mid 1970s and affected adversely the spirit of coexistence that had been built after the establishment of the EEC. The group feeling among member countries began giving way to individual selfish interests, causing the imposition of a new series of regulations and barriers in many member countries. At the same time, socialistic trends gained momentum, especially after Mitterand's Socialist party came in power in France. The economic growth of Germany suffered a setback. A variety of legal barriers were created in France, the Netherlands, and Germany to protect the interests of small, independent retail stores. Strict building and zoning restrictions were introduced in the Netherlands and West Germany. These restrictions hampered large retail corporations with plans to expand their department stores and hyper-markets. Curbs were imposed even on consumer credit extension in the Netherlands.[4] The zoning laws enacted in the United Kingdom did not allow free-standing stores on the ground that they lacked socially redeeming qualities.[5] Retailing firms in Italy, Belgium, and the United Kingdom experienced a great deal of legal harassment because the government favored the growth of small, independent stores. And local zoning boards were a stumbling block in the expansion of many large retail companies, which were left with no alternative but to seek other avenues for growth opportunities. To quote Dr. Dreesmann:

The driving force to internationalization during the last ten years has been the declining prospects in Europe. This caused retailers there to take over or take participations in U.S. and Canadian retailing companies. The grass on this side of the ocean seemed decidedly greener. Nothing has changed in this respect since 1980; on the contrary the outlook for European retailing is dimming by the day."[6]

Legal Environment in Selected Countries

United Kingdom. The legislation that laid the foundation of retail planning at the macrolevel in this country was the Town and Country Planning Act 1948, which introduced a decentralized system of planning under which the local authority was given the responsibility for commerical, industrial, and residential development. At both the country and district level, the local authority was required to develop comprehensive land use plans. Proposals for establishing shopping centers and hypermarkets required specific permission from the local land use planning authority.

The central government ratified the plans of each local authority. Besides the Town and Country Planning Act, the Guidelines of the Ministry of Environment, issued in June 1972, also seek to regulate the expansion of retail business.

West Germany. In West Germany, the Federal Ministry of Economy cooperates with the small business-sponsored Central Association of German Retailers to impose restrictions on the expansion of large department stores and shopping centers. The National Physical Planning Act of 1960 provided the regulatory base for retailing activity in this country. With the amendments made in 1968, the location of regional shopping centers and self-service department stores has been subjected to special area legislation, instituted to control and even hamper the establishment of such shopping facilities.[7] Local zoning boards approve proposals for the expansion of retail stores and the establishment of hypermarkets. Significant amendments to the law were made in 1976 and 1977, integrating local zoning plans into urban plans and putting in specific terms that the applications for building permits for stores with a floor area above 1,500 square meters were likely to be refused if they were located outside central shopping areas. The programs of central area redevelopment and environmental improvement exercised considerable influence on the growth of retailing activity in Germany.

The growth of regional shopping centers in Germany was opposed by downtown department stores. Public policy remained pro-small business for a long time and thus failed to respond to significant social changes taking place in Germany: the emergence of an affluent middle and upper class living on the outskirts of large towns and cities. It hampered the process of modernization of the retail trade, though the market share of large modern retail institutions like department stores, chains, and mail order houses was gradually increasing. A sort of department store-specialty store cartel remained in operation for a long time under the umbrella of restrictive statutes, though it did not work effectively and failed to survive.

Belgium. Public policy in Belgium underwent significant changes to help the growth of retailing geared to the middle class, with the enactment of the Vanden Boeynants Law of May 1959, the promotion of consumer cooperatives, and a curb on the expansion of large stores through several padlock laws enacted from 1936 to 1961. According to Boddewyn, the modernization of Belgian retailing was delayed considerably by such laws.[8] Established small and medium-sized retailers in Belgium viewed new market institutions as a threat to the existing market structure, and the government frequently sided with them in this matter. This resulted at times in considerable legal harrassment of large retail companies when they wanted to expand. The power to zone for commercial purposes shifted from municipalities to provincial and national authorities through the laws of March 29, 1962, and December 22, 1970. In fact there was no effective land use planning in Belgium until 1962.

Earlier, in 1954, a separate ministry, the Ministry for the Middle Classes, was formed to safeguard the interests of small and medium-sized retailers. The growth of large retail establishments was further regulated by the laws of June 11, 1971, and June 29, 1975 (figure 5.1). The 1971 Law on Commerical Practices required retail companies to provide detailed information on prices, quality, and size of product to the government. It sought to create higher standards and more efficiency throughout the retailing system. The growth of superstores and large shopping centers in the early 1970s forced the government to enact the law of June 29, 1975, which sought to control major changes in retail land use and restrain further development of large shopping facilities.

The Ministry of Economic Affairs and the Ministry of Public Works were also involved in supervising the development of large-scale retailing. The prevailing legal framework did not permit the opening of new department stores with five or more employees in towns with less than 50,000 population. This made it very difficult for large retailers to complete their growth programs on schedule. One of the top executives in a large Belgian grocery chain deplored the long bureaucratic procedure in Belgium, which required three to four ministries to make decisions on such matters as the relocation of a store.

Netherlands. There was not much regulation in the Netherlands until 1962 when the Physical Planning Act was passed, which required specific plans to be prepared at the national, regional, and local levels. The Ministry of Physical Planning became the final authority to approve development plans pertaining to large-scale retailing. All new proposals were required to be backed up by retail planning research including socioeconomic surveys and a survey of existing retail structures. The planning research was made mandatory for most regional and local plans. During the 1960s and early 1970s, many urban renewal projects became the target of new planning activity. The new housing schemes were required to contain detailed estimates of shopping floor space requirements for different categories of consumer goods and different levels of shopping centers.

The government is concerned with maintaining a balance between downtown and suburban shopping centers, accomplished by "intensifying the reconstruction of downtown areas, locating new shopping centers in such a manner as to avoid siphoning off downtown business and, generally speaking, avoiding excessive competition between the various clusterings."[9] Such organizations as the Central Board for Retail Trade and Economic Institute for Medium and Small Business help in the implementation of the policy. General legislation introduced in 1976 requires each province to have a retail plan, giving in precise terms the present location, function, and structure of retail trade and information about expected developments.

France. In France, public policy toward retailing reflects a concern for maintaining a balance between small and large commercial organizations.

Figure 5.1
Legislative Process for the Law of 29 June 1975

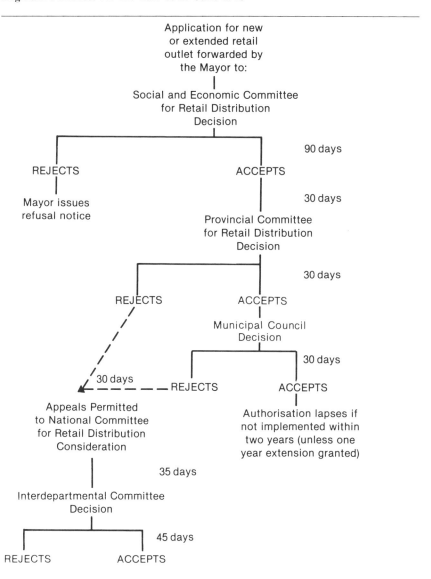

SOURCE: Ross L. Davies, ed., *Retail Planning in the European Community* (Farnborough, Eng.: Gower Publishing Company, 1979), p. 117.

The government favored a slowing down of the spread of large-surface stores and took measures to enhance the conceptual and financial resources of small and medium-sized enterprises to facilitate their transition into larger-sized stores. The Loi Royer set of decrees and orders, introduced in the early 1970s, is believed to be the most comprehensive set of regulatory measures taken by France regarding retail planning. Of special significance was the circular of May 27, 1970, which required that all projects with a provision for selling space in excess of 3,000 square meters be submitted to the committees, and the projects initiated by shopkeepers' associations would be considered favorably.

In France, independent shopkeepers wield a strong political power. Their fight resulted in the law of July 13, 1972, which sought to protect independent shopkeepers. For example, the law requires large-scale retailers to offer financial assistance to elderly shopkeepers wishing to retire.

The regulatory measures of the early 1970s led to the creation of such statutory bodies as the Commercial Urban Planning Commission. The Ministry of Equipment and the Ministry of Economy and Finance are represented on the Central Board, which gives opinions on projects for which no agreement or decision can be reached at the regional level.

Italy. In Italy, it is almost impossible for a new venture to move into retailing if it poses a threat to small retail stores. Law 426, passed in 1971, and Law 73-1193, passed in December 1973, were especially aimed at regulating the growth of large retail establishments. These laws laid down an integrated policy that helped the modernization of retailing systems and ensured coordination in the growth of small and large retail stores. Under these laws, each town council prepares plans for the development and rationalization of retailing systems. All proposals for new store openings, extensions, and relocations need to be approved by the local government. The town council authorizes the operations of large units with a sales area of over 400 square meters selling consumer goods, such as supermarkets, department, stores, variety stores, and hypermarkets.

Major retail projects, those involving stores with a sales area of over 1,500 square meters, have to be approved by the town council and the regional government. Approval is based on project evaluation from the standpoint of its consistency with retail plan forecasts, the impact on the growth of the central area, on employment, and on the overall supply of retailing services regarding demand for these services.[10]

Conclusion. These general laws have had a significant impact on the establishment of new retail stores in most West European countries. The legal environment is particularly harsh in France, Belgium, the Netherlands, and Italy. In addition, there are laws especially focused on advertising, sales promotion, and retail operations. Comparison advertising, allowed in the United States since 1978, is still rare in many European countries. Advertisers in these countries remain vulnerable to lawsuits if they try to establish the superiority of their brand vis-à-vis a competing brand in an advertisement. Advertisers in Italy are forbidden to use common words such as *deodorant* and *perspiration* in television commercials. In Austria, advertising media are subject to taxation, varying from 10 percent to 30 percent of the cost of an insertion from media to media and state to state. The fiscal policy thus alters the cost ratio of various media.

Germany has an extensive and complex regulation of advertising. The Law against Unfair Competition is a significant legal measure that regulates the marketing practices of retailers in Germany. The use of outdoor signs and highway advertising is severely restricted. Retailers normally are not allowed to hold special sales except anniversary sales or end-of-season sales. Germany's cartel act, however, permits manufactures to exercise in certain situations discrimination in the choice of their customers. Even price discrimination is considered legal on the ground that it provides an important stimulus to competition.

Many European countries do not allow commercials on radio or television. In Britain, as in the United States, cigarettes, and liquor cannot be advertised on television. Moreover, many countries have laid down regulations on promotional practices like contests, deals, free offers, and premiums.

The laws in some countries control the discount that can be given at retail and require permits for all sales promotions. France prohibits door-to-door selling. Sometimes health and sanitary regulations have come in the way of large-scale retailing. In Switzerland, dairy products are not allowed to be sold with other merchandise in self-service grocery stores. These local laws are designed to safeguard the interests of small dairy product retailers.

In Belgium, the law of 14 July, 1971, sought to protect consumers against unfair practices or promotions, such as selling below cost, liquidation sales, clearance sales, selling at reduced prices, premiums, and offers of coupons or stamps. Similar laws were enacted in France during the early 1970s, after the initial successful entry of supermarkets in the 1950s and hypermarkets in the 1960s. The competition between large retail stores and traditional small and medium-sized firms has led at times to commercial practices that need to be curbed. The Ministry of Economy and Finance published a circular on May 30, 1970, interpreting and regulating "profitless sales," "special prices," and "publicizing reduced prices." Special laws in the Netherlands set rules and limits on such practices as special gifts, price reductions and stamps, shop closures, and clearance.

Population Trends

From the standpoint of population growth, European markets were not considered to be very promising. Birthrates in West European countries had been declining steadily since the mid-1960s. Family life-styles had undergone important changes in these countries: a preference for later marriage, widespread use of contraceptives, liberalized abortion and divorce laws, and the increased number of working women.

The year 1965 marked the beginning of a steep fall in birthrates in most European countries, except Ireland and Greece, resulting in a slower overall population growth in Europe. Europe's share of the global population is expected to decline from 10.8 percent in 1970 to 8.4 percent in 1990. The trend will have a lesser impact in southern Europe, where annual increases are expected to continue around 1.5 percent. Some northern European countries have already reached the level of less than zero population growth. For example, the population of West Germany has been declining steadily since 1972, reaching the level of 57 million in 1981. It fell by 100,000 in 1977 alone and is expected to reach 52 million by the year 2000.

Another important reason for population decline in many countries has been the slowdown in net immigration due to high unemployment levels.

Based on current trends, the populations of France, Belgium, Sweden, and Switzerland are expected to start falling within a few years. Austria, Norway, and Denmark are at zero population growth level and may soon move toward a negative growth rate.[11] This decline in population trend was another dampening effect on the growth-oriented European companies.

ORGANIZATIONAL OR MICROLEVEL FACTORS

The macrolevel factors impelled many large European retailers to perceive and exploit new growth opportunites elsewhere, particularly in the United States, which offered a number of compatibilities in the realm of ethnicity, language, climate, religion, and the level of industrial development. Most fast-growing firms in Europe found themselves in the late 1960s and early 1970s in a state of stagnation, or corporate claustrophobia, because the domestic market had saturated and the growth vector offered nothing so attractive or challenging in the domestic market. Otto Versand, Europe's third largest mail-order house, considered strong competition and diminished sales horizons in Europe as one of the important motivations for its buying the major U.S. mail-order company, Spiegel.[12] Others also started experiencing an acute need for relocating capital to generate higher return on investment and for exploring growth opportunities in new types of retailing. Some felt the need for self-defense against the possibility of being acquired by another company and decided in favor of horizontal market extension to insulate themselves. However, a major internal stimulus was provided by the need to select a suitable portfolio overseas to absorb accumulated profits.

The worsening economic situation and the stifling legal environment prevailing in Europe during the 1960s and early 1970s led most large business firms to adopt a strategy of planned growth. Corporate managements began to realize the importance of programs of growth and expansion.

Mergers and acquisitions began to be considered effective means of securing new portfolios, which would ensure sustained corporate growth. Their interest in U.S. retail companies can be explained by the large size of the U.S. market, its potential buying power, and the lesser vulnerability of its retail industry to recessionary trends. Indeed the industry had shown an impressive growth during the 1960s and 1970s, which made most European companies interested in acquiring a potentially sound retail operation in the United States rather than going through the time-consuming process of starting a new enterprise. The process was expedited when stocks were available at attractive rates and the owners of U.S. companies were themselves interested in friendly takeovers.

One top executive in a leading Dutch retail enterprise said that his company decided to move ahead when it found a chain of stores in the United States compatible with one of its European chains in terms of store type, merchandise mix, and market segment. Top management expected to see synergistic results from such compatible acquisitions. They believed that a planned growth through merger and acquisition was the only way to combat a situation of cost inflation outpacing the inflation of consumer goods retail prices. This was not an unusual situation in many countries where prices of essential food items were under close government surveillance.

A dominant position in a domestic market with a large market share was another factor that made some European companies go overseas. For example, a leading retail company in the Netherlands not only held a strong position in the domestic retail trade and service sector, but its yearly rate of growth exceeded that of the Dutch economy as a whole. The group was therefore obliged to divert part of its expansion elsewhere lest countervailing powers harm it.[13]

Most European companies that made investments in U.S. retailing had experience in various types of retailing in their home country, as well as in other countries in Europe and even Latin America. Understanding the dynamics of U.S. retailing, they probably decided to move into this market after they had attained some maturity and self-confidence. What is interesting to observe is that most companies chose the path of horizontal rather than vertical market integration. They maintained their primary involvement in retailing or closely related processing industries and did not consider other industries as avenues of investment or capital relocation. When asked to explain this phenomenon, one executive said that they were in the market for the consumer dollar. In an already risky and competitive business environment, they could not think of staking their resources in unfamiliar or nonrelated fields. They felt more confident and secure by directing their investments to an industry that had not only given them the basic strength but had also remained relatively less vulnerable to technological outgrowth or recessionary downturn.

Learning Retailing Skills

The opportunity to learn new retail skills was also an important motivation. New retailing ideas had been emerging in the United States and flowing across the Atlantic for several decades now; retailing in Europe had always lagged behind. Although the learning of new skills was not perceived to be the primary objective of these investments, it turned out to be a worthwhile secondary objective. Most investors had a keen eye on what the new acquisition could contribute to the improvement of European operations: what new techniques could be brought home and, in turn, what could be given back to the U.S. operations. My interviews revealed that some European aspirants carefully selected for acquisition targets that appeared to be good candidates for the adoption of a European formula. Contrary to apparent expectations of environmental gaps, in some cases a U.S.-based convenience store presented a business and cultural outlook more compatible to one based in Zurich than to one located across the border, say in Karlsruhe, West Germany.

A Dutch group, for example, had anticipated an exchange of know-how as a result of collaboration with foreign retailers. A recent report published by this group said that this cooperation led "to enriching the Group's experience and to starting completely new learning curves. In other countries, this cooperation leads to exchange of know-how, in which it is sometimes the Dutch partner who contributes more to the local management. Synergistic advantages can be observed which result from the cooperation between specialized retailing businesses abroad, which are either fully owned by the Group or in which the Group has a participation."[14]

Readiness for Entry in the United States

The European companies had equipped themselves well in terms of manpower and experience to enter the U.S. market. Many had acquired experience with foreign operations on and outside the Continent before they moved into the United States. During the 1960s and 1970s, moreover, they had greatly expanded their managerial capabilities, financial resources, and research orientation.[15] Through working for the U.S. firms or in competing firms and having studied in U.S. educational institutions, foreign managers had developed suitable managerial skills. Therefore it was not difficult for many of them to assume key positions in the newly acquired U.S. retail companies. Delhaize, for example, had accumulated considerable experience in foreign retailing in Spain before it acquired its interest in Food Town, and Alterman and C&A Brenninkmeyers had set up specialty stores in Brazil before moving to the United States.

The European aspirants nevertheless entered the game rather cautiously and contracted out preinvestment surveys and marketing research to U.S.-based investment brokerage firms and, in some cases, their European branches and industry associations such as the Food Marketing Institute. Some hired leading public relations and advertising agencies to produce supportive published material that would facilitate their entry and assimilation to the U.S. economy.

When they started reviewing suitable acquisition candidates in the United States, many European companies discovered several good firms, some in the midst of severe financial crisis, looking for new sources of funds to salvage themselves, as well as to boost the morale of their employees and creditors. Others were financially secure but had reached a point of saturation where further growth was possible only through radical changes in corporate strategy. In a few cases, the European investors found some good retail operations that were looking for successors to top management and therefore wanting to sell the business.

When asked what they basically looked for when they wanted to invest in U.S. retailing, one chief executive of a French retail chain mentioned the following as their basic concerns over and above the level of stock prices:

1. Possibility of a friendly acquisition

2. Structure of shareholding

3. Good management team

4. Established company with a record of consistent profitability

5. Type of retail institution less vulnerable to economic recession such as conventional grocery store or a convenience 7-11 type store

6. Location in a sunbelt state

In some cases, Europeans invested in companies in poor financial condition when they found that the poor performance was the result of the indifference and negligence on the part of the corporate management of the parent company. A Swiss company, for example, found a large U.S. corporation unable to give adequate parental support to one of its possessions, a chain of toy stores with good growth potential. The Swiss company decided to acquire this chain because of its long experience in the toy business, its cordial relationship with the American corporation that owned the chain, and its confidence that it could turn the business around. After the acquisition, the Swiss company revamped the organizational structure, introduced modernized office systems, and built a dependable management team.

Experience in the U.S. market and the opportunity executives had for receiving a college education in the U.S. proved useful to many European companies. The younger generation in the families of the pioneers like the Brenninkmeyers, Hugo Mann, Franz Carl Weber, and Agache Willot received their education in leading U.S. business schools. Erivan Haub, chief of Tengelmann Group, had working experience in such well-known U.S. chains as the Jewel Company (Chicago) and Alpha Beta (California) before the Tengelmann group acquired the majority interest in A&P.

Thus, the U.S. market provided a number of compatibilities in culture, language, nationality, level of economic growth, terrain, and climate. It also offered in abundance what the European companies missed most at home—a vast landscape and an economy that valued free enterprise and equality of opportunity.

Investment candidates in the United States also preferred takeovers by outside foreign companies. In some cases, the entrepreneurs or founders were ready to retire and wanted to hand over the business to capable hands. They were particularly encouraged to do so when the prospective buyers were more interested in making a good investment and apparently had no intention to interfere in the existing management style, policies, and programs. Thus, top management in the candidate U.S. companies saw in foreign offers a twofold promise: the promise of financial revitalization and the promise of retaining the individual identity of the chain intact. There was always a risk of losing identity and degenerating into a small division in the event a retail chain was acquired by a large domestic corporation like Coca-Cola or W. R. Grace. Thus, the chief executives in the affected U.S. retail chains saw better prospects for maintaining the status quo (including their own job) with the ownership being transferred to Europe, rather than to a large domestic company.

The other interest of acquisition candidates was the assurance of capital inflow that was badly needed to finance long-overdue expansion programs. The acquisition of Grand Union by Cavenham U.S.A. (Générale Occidentale S.A., Paris) was prompted by the former's urgent need for funds. To finance the capital projects, Sir James Goldsmith acquired $183 million in capital for Grand Union by selling his British holdings in Allied Suppliers and simultaneously reducing his French holdings in U.S. hardware stores. Concerned about the prevailing socialist policies of the French government, Sir Goldsmith was believed to be gradually transferring control of his enterprises from the French holding company to another holding in Hong Kong, Générale Oriental.[16]

Thus, two sets of factors—one emanating from the European countries, called push factors, and the other emanating from the United States, called pull factors—were instrumental in accelerating the trend of European acquisitions witnessed since the early 1970s. The push factors included macrolevel environmental factors such as the economic decline and political changes seen in many European countries, overcrowding and resultant cut-throat competition among retail business firms, and stiffer planning and zoning laws enacted in many countries that ran counter to the expansion and growth programs of leading retail firms. The government in many countries joined with traditional retailing institutions to prevent the modernization of retailing and slow down the growth of such companies that were moving ahead to respond to emerging socioeconomic forces. The push factors also included internal or microlevel factors such as the saturation point reached by many companies, resulting in their need for new directions for growth, their need for spreading the risks, and for exchanging trading and managerial skills with U.S. firms.

On the other hand, a series of pull factors directed the inflow of capital from Europe to the United States. The macrolevel pull factors included depreciation of the U.S. dollar, a depressed stock market, and appreciating values of real estate, a stable political and economic system, and a benign legal environment, relative to many European countries, which did not make any discrimination against foreign investors. There were also some microlevel pull factors, such as the availability of certain retail companies at a good price and easy identification of some firms that needed a quick turnaround, where reorganization was long overdue and where capital projects were awaiting implementation.

The matching of these push and pull factors was facilitated by several sociocultural compatibilities between the regions, as shown in figure 5.2.

NOTES

1. U.S. Department of Commerce, International Trade Administration, *Attracting Foreign Investment to the United States* (Washington D.C., Government Printing Office, 1981), pp. 1-7.

2. "Brothers Who Want Korvettes," *New York Times*, February 4, 1979, sec. 3, pp. 1-7.

3. For a comprehensive discussion on environmental motivations of foreign investors in U.S. business, see U.S. Department of Commerce, *Foreign Direct Investment in the United States, Report of the Secretary of Commerce to the Congress* (April 1976), 1:97-111.

4. "Vroom, Vroom," *Economist*, January 12, 1980, p. 74.

5. "British Supermarkets Turn to Non-Foods More and More," *Chain Store Age Executive* (May 1980):115.

6. Speech delivered by A. C. R. Dreesmann to the Annual Convention of National Retail Merchants Association, held in Toronto, April 1982.

7. J. J. Boddewyn and S. C. Hollander, *Public Policy toward Retailing* (Lexington, Mass.: Lexington Books, 1972), p. 414.

8. Ibid., p. 45.

9. Ibid., p. 258.

10. Ross L. Davies, ed., *Retail Planning in the European Community* (Farnborough, England: Saxon House, 1979), p. 155.

11. *Statistical Yearbook*, 1979/1980 (New York: United Nations, 1981).

12. "German Mail Order Firms Eye U.S.," *Wall Street Journal*, March 2, 1982, p. 35.

13. Vroom & Dreesmann, *Annual Report*, 1980-1981, p. 25.

14. Ibid., p. 25.

15. *Foreign Direct Investment in the United States,* 1: 99.

16. "A Magnet Moves His Empire across the Sea," *Business Week*, May 31, 1982, p. 39.

Figure 5.2
Key Motivational Factors

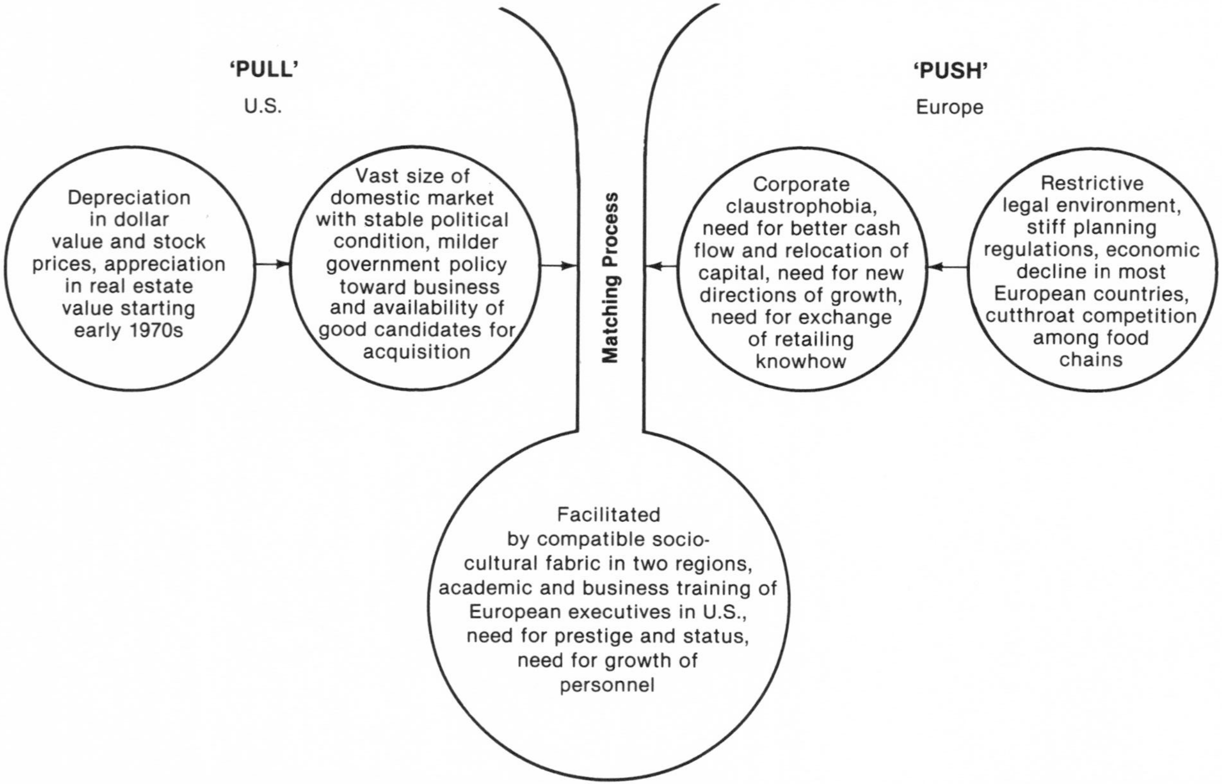

'PULL'
U.S.

'PUSH'
Europe

Matching Process

Depreciation in dollar value and stock prices, appreciation in real estate value starting early 1970s

Vast size of domestic market with stable political condition, milder government policy toward business and availability of good candidates for acquisition

Corporate claustrophobia, need for better cash flow and relocation of capital, need for new directions of growth, need for exchange of retailing knowhow

Restrictive legal environment, stiff planning regulations, economic decline in most European countries, cutthroat competition among food chains

Facilitated by compatible socio-cultural fabric in two regions, academic and business training of European executives in U.S., need for prestige and status, need for growth of personnel

74

6

The Impact of Foreign Investments

What has been the impact of foreign investments at the microlevel and macrolevel? What strategic or organizational changes, if any, have taken place in the affected U.S. company? In case a U.S. retail company did undergo change after acquisition, what was the nature of such a change: routine change that would have occurred anyway or a significant strategic or organizational change made at the initiative of new owners-investors? Have these changes been effective in improving the state of affairs in the affected companies?

The aftermath of European investment could also be viewed at the aggregate or macro-level. Have the acquisitions enhanced the American retail industry in terms of better financial results, greater employment, reduced mortality, import of new retailing know-how and greater satisfaction to the consumer? These questions will be addressed in this chapter.

MICROLEVEL IMPACT

Several foreign acquistions that occurred in the U.S. retail industry created a situation leading to changes in top management, redefinition of organizational objectives, reformulation of strategies and policies, and a time-bound program of turnaround or growth. In some cases, the European parent company preferred an arrangement in which the existing management team in the U.S. affiliate continued to function. A few made such arrangements as a precondition to making investments. In others, the European parents wanted a free hand, and the acquisitions led to a reformulation of business strategy and important changes in top management. The transfer of ownership led to resignations or premature retirement of senior executives, especially where they suspected major changes in or a reversal of the current structure and strategies. Table 6.1 presents some examples of both types of situations.

Table 6.1
CEOs after Acquisition

Where the CEO Continued after Acquisition	Where a New CEO Was Appointed after Acquisition
Jonathan L. Scott, chairman of A&P, continued as chief executive after Tengelmann acquired 42 percent interest there; later replaced by James Wood	Martin S. Kramer, Gimbels' chairman, took early retirement; James A. Connolly, president of Gimbels, resigned. Gimbels and Saks Fifth Avenue were brought under the umbrella of Batus Retail Division with Allan R. Johnson, chairman of Saks, and Robert J. Suslow, president, as top executives. With the acquisition of Marshall Field, Chicago, and following the retirement of Allan Johnson, Robert Suslow was named the division's chairman; Angelo Arena, chairman and chief executive of Marshall Field, was named vice-chairman of the division. Arnold Aronson, chairman of Saks Fifth Avenue, took over as president in place of Robert Suslow
Sol Price continued as chief executive of Fed Mart after the latter's acquisition by Hugo Mann, who assumed the chairmanship	Anthony Brenninkmeyer took over as chairman of Ohrbach's after Nathan Ohrbach left the chairmanship in 1965
Ralph Ketner, president of Food Town Stores, continued to head the operation after Delhaize acquired the majority share in this company	The Cavenhams (U.S.) hired James Wood from U.K. to run Grand Union; Wood later moved to A&P as chief executive
Julian Jackson, chairperson, Lil' Champ, and Harold Kelly, president of Bi-Lo, continued in office after acquisition	David Brous, chief executive of Korvettes, resigned soon after it was taken over by Agache Willot Group, with Alain Mathieu as head of the U.S. subsidiary

Redefinition of Goals and Strategies

Among the companies studied, several were noted for making serious efforts to redefine their objectives, strategies, and trading areas. The new stockholders took the acquisition as a challenge, especially where the U.S. companies had been undergoing serious financial crisis and a turn-around strategy was called for. It is difficult to say, at least from the limited number of cases examined, whether the speculative motives overrode the rational business motives in the decision-making process involved in the acquisition of U.S. retail companies. In most cases, the new management gave the impression that their decisions to invest were based on a careful evaluation of risks and opportunities, and they were going to adopt a fresh approach to problems or formulate new strategies to revitalize the growth of their respective organizations. The change in top management came in natural course in many organizations like Ohrbach's, Batus Retail Division, Grand Union, and Korvettes to give new directions and to initiate and implement programs directed to business growth. Even where the new owners decided to continue with the incumbents at the top level, serious efforts were made to accentuate the profitability growth through stringent cost reduction and improved operating efficiency. This is illustrated by the following cases.

Aftermath of Acquisitions: Brief Cases

A&P. Before being acquired by the Tengelmann Group, A&P had grown into an unwieldy network of over 3,000 stores and a large food manufacturing plant at Horseheads, New York, which produced its private-label food items. The number of stores was considerably reduced to 1,800 by 1979 when the German investors struck the deal. The shares changed hands at one-third of their book value. Tengelmann has since invested over $100 million in the company.

Regardless of the unfavorable reactions of Huntington Hartford, grandson of the founders of A&P, the industrial and financial communities were quite receptive to the acquisition and hailed it as a providential help, especially since previous attempts to revive the chain had failed.

The new management identified serious flaws in the company's manufacturing and marketing functions. They decided to close about 230 stores and sell off many of its manufacturing plants, which had not been doing well. They also realized that the company would not gain much from the survival plan prescribed by leading consultants Booz, Allen & Hamilton. In April 1982, the new management sold the detergent plant at Brockport, New York, to Kleen Brite Laboratories and closed the Horseheads plant. Under the leadership of James Wood, the new chief executive who was brought from the United Kingdom by the Cavenhams to salvage the Grand Union chain, the number of stores was reduced further to 1,543 in 1980, 1,449 in 1981, and 1,020 in 1982 in 26 eastern and southern states.[1]

With Tengelmann's edge in discount selling, Wood began to convert many A&P stores into Plus stores, with merchandise displayed in cardboard boxes and prices posted on signs rather than stamped on individual items. Plus stores thus had low overheads and could break even on sales within a store size of 12,000 square feet. The efforts to sustain Plus stores failed, however, resulting in a loss of $75 million to A&P over a two-year period. James Wood observed on this experiment: "The mistakes we foreigners often make is to judge the U.S. on the basis of what we know about Europe. Americans want a fuller range of products from a supermarket than people on the other side of the water."[2] The company later decided to stop the expansion of nonfrill Plus stores and concentrate on the modernization of A&P stores in key markets.[3] After a long struggle and heavy losses (of the order of $43 million in 1981), A&P showed a positive performance in 1982, giving some assurance to its stockholders that top management's efforts would succeed. It has now embarked upon an expansion program. In 1983, it acquired Milwaukee-based Kohl's Food Stores from Batus Inc. More recently, it acquired 14 Eagle supermarkets from Lucky Stores Inc., Wisconsin and 20 supermarkets in Virginia from Pantry Pride Inc.

Fed Mart. At Fed Mart, Hugo Mann, the new chairman, indicated his company's interest in converting some stores into hypermarkets modeled on their Wertkauf stores in Germany. Upon acquisition, the new management planned to invest $7.5 million and make an additional investment of $25 million in equity to accomplish this goal. They also invested $57 million out of profits. Between 1977 and 1979, several changes were made in the management; some stores were remodeled and the merchandise mix suitably altered to convert them into hypermarkets.[4] The company ran into numerous problems in the course of implementing its program. In 1979, it had sales of nearly $1,000 million but failed to make any profit. It continued to show losses until January 1981 and was later turned into a private company by its chairman and majority stockholder, Hugo Mann. The same year, the company decided to close down operations.

Red Food. Promodes (Mondiville, France) acquired the ownership of Red Food Stores, a grocery chain operating in Tennessee and northern Georgia, in January 1980. The French company's move to the United States was considered to be an extension of what it had already started as a strategic move in the international markets. The parent organization adopted a policy of minimal interference in the U.S. operations: a decentralized approach, leaving the entire decision-making process in the hands of local management and a small group of parent company executives. The U.S. chain had long needed strategic planning for future growth, and its stockholders opted for an outside ownership that could inject new investments as well as point in new directions. The transfer of ownership almost synchronized with the retirement of Red Food's chief executive. The arrival of a new chief executive, with long experience in similar grocery chains in the South, facilitated the change. Red Food Stores have since been growing steadily, moving toward higher productivity and showing improved financial performance. A strategic plan is underway for enlarging and expanding the existing stores, adding new stores, revamping the storage and warehousing system, and establishing a marketing information system.

Bi-Lo. Another leading grocery chain headquartered in South Carolina, Bi-Lo has been undergoing a program of expansion and renovation since its acquisition by Ahold N.V., Netherlands, in August 1977. The chain operates over 140 stores, mainly in North and South Carolina and Georgia. The previous chief executive of this chain decided to quit when top management wanted to sell beer and wine in some of the stores. Subsequent to acquisition, several noteworthy changes were made in the company. The distribution center went through a massive renovation, with technical assistance from the parent company. Other areas that received emphasis after the acquisition were personnel development, marketing research, and the information system. Top management set up a well-equipped training facility in the corporate headquarters that took care of the training needs of various levels of store personnel. Specialists were hired to create a new visual image that reflected more closely the progressive character of the organization.[5] Many stores have been remodeled and expanded, with a new decor, equipment replacement, and new beverage departments. Eight new stores were opened during the first half of 1982. As in several other cases, the change in ownership led the executives of this company to spell out their mission and objectives. Figure 6.1 shows how Bi-Lo perceives its mission, strategy, and objectives.

Spiegel. Early in 1982, Otto Versand GmbH, Europe's third largest mail-order firm, acquired Spiegel, one of the largest mail-order companies in the United States. "We've already covered the European market and it was time for a jump over the Atlantic"; this is how the chairman, Michael Otto, hailed the company's decision. The German company is using caution in the new venture to avoid the consequences it witnessed in the case of A&P and Fed Mart.[6]

The German mail-order house attributes its European expansion to three key factors: wide assortment of merchandise, fast delivery, and good customer service. According to Otto, the company analyzed several companies in the United States for a number of years and narrowed the number down until they decided on Spiegel. As far as their business strategy was concerned, they planned only limited changes. "We'd be very careful in changing the marketing system because it is an American system," said Otto. "We'd bring in things on the management side because these are systems that can be applied internationally."[7] Spiegel might try such European innovations as using local sales representatives who work in their own neighborhoods and use of specialized catalogs. The parent companies expect that in the future, more similarities will develop between European

Figure 6.1
BI-LO: Mission, Strategy, and Objectives

BI-LO
Its Mission . . . Its Strategy . . . Its Objectives

A successful company must define its *mission*.

Once that mission is defined the company must develop an overall *strategy* or broad plan to guide it toward completion of the mission.

Within the strategy are short, medium, or long-range tactical *objectives* which are building blocks, or stepping stones, toward making the strategy effective.

If those objectives are met, the strategy is fulfilled, and the mission is accomplished.

When you, as a member of the BI-LO organization, are the implementer of even a single tactic, *you* are totally involved in fulfilling the overall strategy and in accomplishing the mission.

The words above are a concise guide for success in any business, but for them to be meaningful and beneficial to us, we have to apply them to BI-LO.

To do this we would ask ourselves three basic questions. These questions are:

What is BI-LO's mission?
What is BI-LO's strategy?
What are BI-LO's objectives?

The purpose of this message is to communicate the answers to these questions as clearly as possible.

The next purpose is to *solicit the help of the individual member* of the BI-LO organization in accomplishing the mission of BI-LO and state the company's *role in supporting your efforts.*

The BI-LO Mission

"To operate supermarkets which attract and serve an ever-broadening segment of the people in our marketing area; and to operate these stores on a profitable basis."

Inherent in this mission statement is the determination to widen the appeal of BI-LO and accelerate the in-flow of new customers by providing a service which will meet the needs of shoppers of all ages, background, family sizes and income groups.

The BI-LO Strategy

"To promise and deliver maximum value for money by offering consistent quality merchandise at the lowest prices in our marketing area; and at all times to provide a shopping atmosphere of the highest standard characterized by cleanliness, friendliness and service."

The BI-LO Objectives

- "To continue the aggressive growth of BI-LO through new store development: (during 1982 approximately twenty new stores will be added to the company for a total of one hundred and fifty stores. Similar growth is anticipated in the years 1983, 1984, and thereafter); to penetrate east Tennessee as the fourth state of BI-LO operations.
- "To operate the cleanest stores, supplemented by an informed and friendly organization to achieve maximum customer satisfaction; to provide a continuing improvement in earning capability and employee benefits to the BI-LO organization.
- "To provide the finest quality meat in our marketing areas."
- "To establish BI-LO as the number one produce merchant in its marketing area."

- "To provide, through the newly formed Management Development Department, opportunities for the development of the BI-LO organization and its people; to provide training programs, educational opportunities and support, and career development for all levels of BI-LO employees."
- "To upgrade all stores through a continuing remodel and equipment replenishment program to provide the highest image of BI-LO to its customers and potential customers."
- "To continually monitor the ever-changing needs of customers, their buying habits and desires, and their economic needs; to provide these needs at the lowest prices in the BI-LO marketing area."
- "To provide the service requirements for our stores consistent with control of our cost of doing business."
- "To continually recognize that the most important asset to BI-LO is its human resources; to be fully cognizant that BI-LO's success is consistent with the success of its employees."

The above is a brief summary of our mission, our strategy, and our objectives. The future is bright for BI-LO and the security and well-being for the future can be further ensured for all of the BI-LO organization if we devote our unified efforts in the achievement of these objectives.

This effort is epitomized by this saying:

Look To This Day!
Yesterday is but a Dream
And Tomorrow is only a Vision:
But Today well-lived makes
Every Yesterday a Dream of
Happiness.
And every Tomorrow a Vision
of Hope.

With kind personal regards
Lawson Saul

and American tastes, leading to an increase in world-wide styling and more opportunities for business growth.

Grand Union. Grand Union was acquired by the Cavenham Group (U.K.) in the early 1970s, financed by the grandparent holding company, Générale Occidentale, S.A., of France. The British parent company hired James Wood to manage the affairs of this famous chain, which, like A&P, had grown too big and unwieldy. Top management decided to adopt a three-pronged approach to save Grand Union: close down unprofitable stores, change the merchandise mix, and tighten the financial reporting.[8] It decided to concentrate within selected market areas, launch a major store conversion and renovation program, and convert its core operations from conventional supermarkets to full-service Food Markets and Food Centers. The number of stores has been reduced significantly from 856 at the end of 1980 to 610 in April, 1983. This reduction, as well as the implementation of a new strategy, has adversely affected the sales and net income of the company, but the company is quite optimistic about its future.

The company has been converting its high-volume and most profitable supermarkets into Food Markets in the 40,000 to 50,000 square foot range. It has been experimenting with several new departments such as Sweet Spot, featuring an assortment of domestic and foreign candies; Cookie Heaven, featuring its own high-quality cookies; Taste Place, a specialty food island; and the Cooks' Harvest, which offers some 200 varieties of natural foods displayed in bulk. During 1982, the company invested $116 million in its capital program, said to be the highest in the company's history, as part of its six-year capital development program.

Batus Inc. The Brown & Williamson Group, formed as Batus Inc. in 1980, decided to place Kohl, Gimbels, and Saks Fifth Avenue under one umbrella, designated as the Retail Division of Batus Inc. It launched in 1979 a massive $200 million expansion program for Saks, which provided for a plan to open two new stores a year. The marketing approach for Saks has been broadened to appeal to younger or younger-minded customers.[9] The strategy for Gimbels was set in terms of "getting out of unprofitable hard goods and renovating many of its older stores."

For the early 1980s, Batus had planned a large capital investment on the order of $70.2 million for opening new stores and for renovating and creating support facilities. Funds have been allocated for updating of selected Gimbels stores. Management has continued efforts in critical areas such as productivity, cost control, and inventory planning to improve the performance of Gimbels and Kohl's food stores. Five new stores were added to the Saks Fifth Avenue chain, and four new stores joined the group of Kohl's specialty chain during 1981-1983.[10]

The financial results of Batus Retailing Group for 1983 showed a 31 percent gain in operating profit and a 27 percent gain in sales. The total sales of its eleven retail divisions crossed the $3 billion mark. The group opened 15 new stores in 1983 representing an additional 1,100,000 square feet of floor space. It has made plans to invest more than $50 million in Marshall Field and achieve $4 billion of sales by 1985.[11]

Korvettes. Agache Willot, the new owner of Korvettes, made a series of changes in the strategies, organization, and personnel. In its bid to turn around the trouble-stricken organization, it decided to disband the "Other Korvettes" campaign introduced by its predecessors and tried to position the store between a discount store and a department store. The new chairman, Alain Mathieu, announced that his main objective was "to improve the profits—by being better retailers, cleaning up our inventories, becoming more competitive, motivating our people better and increasing store productivity."[12]

Assessment. It is difficult to say whether changes in top management or in managerial strategies have resulted in increased revenues and income. Some of the retail companies acquired by Europeans are still struggling to get out of the red, let alone show some respectable results. A&P, after a long struggle and heavy losses (approximately $43 million in 1981), was able to show some positive results in 1982. Fed Mart faced serious problems and decided to close down in 1981, with losses exceeding $6 million.[13] Food Giant recorded a loss of $2.8 million in 1981. Retail operations of British parents—Grand Union, Gimbels, and Saks Fifth Avenue, among others—have been showing strength, but with the exception of Saks Fifth Avenue, the pace of growth remains slow. According to recent press reports, both Gimbels/New York and Gimbels/Philadelphia have turned the corner after many years in the red.[14] In fact, the years 1980 and 1981 were poor for the industry as a whole, and it would be unfair to attribute such performance to European ownership alone. Nevertheless, many of these companies have taken too long to move from transition to stability. Korvettes succumbed within two years of takeover. And the results were not too encouraging when some European parents experimented, such as A&P's no-frill Plus stores, Fed Mart's hypermarkets modeled on Wertkauf stores in Germany, and Mothercare's maternity shops.

Organizational Identity

Have these acquisitions helped to maintain the acquired company's identity, or does it get lost in the process? Both types of consequences are possible. The acquisitions of relatively smaller food chains located mostly in the sunbelt states were welcomed by local management because the corporate identity of these chains remained intact. On the other hand, acquistions by large groups like Batus Inc. affected the identity of such well-known companies as Gimbels Brothers and Marshall Field, which were sometimes grouped with others under one umbrella.

With the acquisition of Marshall Field, the Batus retail division went through a major restructuring that paved the way for tighter control and possible divestiture of weaker divisions. According to one press report, "Marshall Field & Co. is gone forever. The corporate entity that Chairman Angelo Arena dreamed would become a national retailer and ensure his place in merchandising history, was dismantled by its new owners."[15]

The chief executive of one discount food chain observed while reflecting over the future plans of his organization that his chain would need to trade up a bit in the quality of merchandise mix and customer profile. It hired the services of a leading consultant to create a new visual identity that more accurately reflected its progressive, fast-growing enterprise.

MACROLEVEL IMPACT

Transfer of Retail Technology

The long-run effect of foreign acquisitions on the U.S. economy is evident by looking at the net gains of technology transfer. According to a Department of Commerce study on foreign direct investment in the United States, most foreign owners were motivated to acquire U.S companies to gain first-hand knowledge of marketing techniques, and the net flow of technology in this area appeared to be outward. When confined to the retail sector, it is difficult to judge the validity of this conclusion reached in the study. U.S. retailing techniques related to product assortment, financial controls, merchandising controls, warehousing, and visual displays have been adopted by European countries. At the same time, European investors, including Hugo Mann, Tengelmann, and the Albrecht Group, made attempts to try certain innovations apparently successful in Europe such as hypermarkets, Plus discount stores, and no-frill box stores, respectively. These were not very successful in the United States. Other European investors claimed in the course of interviews that they applied new management techniques in the acquired U.S. chains and helped them in a number of ways by improving their organizational structure through the hiring of new personnel, replacement of old equipment, creation of more effective distribution systems, and relocation of unprofitable stores. Interviews with senior executives in Europe and the United States revealed different patterns of the exchange of retailing know-how across the Atlantic.

The chief executive of a Brussels-based company commented that the company hoped to introduce new techniques and systems in its recently acquired U.S. affiliates, such as retail planning and budgetary systems and recruitment of more capable personnel. Management also hoped for a fruitful exchange of retailing know-how—for example, transferring to the United States techniques in the areas of buying, storage, and merchandising of fresh produce and other perishables and getting in exchange from the United States better retailing techniques in the areas of dry grocery, cooling and heating technologies, and others.

A chief executive of a Swiss-based toy retailer lamented the fact that the toy chain it had acquired in the United States was financially weak and had been poorly managed for a long time prior to acquisition. He strongly believed that the acquisition had resulted in an improvement in organizational efficiency. Management anticipated significant changes in the toy business in view of the changing size of age groups of children and planned to make innovations that included the introduction of game boutiques. The company deplored the philosophy of most U.S. retailers, who view warehousing and retailing as two separate functions and prefer to invest only in the latter. The European company, on the other hand, believes in the interdependence of these two functions and therefore shows more concern for effective logistics systems.

The chief executive of a Dutch group of retail companies made another claim for the contribution his group could make to the U.S. retail industry. Companies in the Netherlands, he observed, are used to working under severe environmental pressures and are concerned about raising productivity. They endeavor to accomplish this through rigorous discipline in the matter of assortment, internal layout, planning, and organization. The previous owners of their U.S. affiliate paid little attention to these areas; their major interest was limited to the market value of investment. When the Dutch company was examining various proposals, it found a variety store chain that matched in merchandise mix and target market with one of its chains in the Netherlands and decided to acquire it in the hope of realizing synergistic gains. The new management hoped that eventually they would introduce private brands in the U.S. chain as they did in the Netherlands by buying merchandise from the Far East.

A French investor in a Florida-based convenience store chain was optimistic about the inflow of modern retailing practices through its U.S. acquisition. The French company had made only a minority acquisition but nevertheless had initiated the process of long-range planning to make the U.S. operation more viable.

A Dutch company, somewhat conservative in orientation, believed that the exchange of retailing know-how would be more to its advantage because it had acquired an aggressive food discounter with a record of good merchandising and customer service.

Several European investors claimed that the acquired U.S. retail companies lacked sound organization, professional management, planned growth programs, and employee morale. The aftermath of acquisition in many cases was noted for the fresh look management gave to these critical factors. The new management at some retail companies hired professionals who made use of financial ratios and created separate departments for employee development and management information. Various types of in-store innovations, such as a self-service meat department, computerized cash registers, and imported food lines, were noted in some of the recently acquired grocery stores. In a few cases, the European parent company sent experts to help the U.S. affiliate in implementing major organizational changes. One was found to be involved periodically in conducting consumer and store studies and another in helping the U.S. chain in the modernization and expansion of its central warehouse facility.

In the case of one relatively successful department store chain in the United States, the involvement of European investors was found to be minimal, confined to their representation in one or two administrative committees. The chief executive of the European company said that it preferred staying away from the day-to-day operations of the U.S company and followed a policy of least interference.

Thus, discussions with executives in the United States and Europe indicated that most acquisitions led to a significant improvement in the operational efficiency of the acquired U.S. retail companies. However, it is difficult to conclude whether the United States benefited from retailing innovations brought from Europe. The European investors had little new to share with their U.S. counterparts. One of their main goals was to have a testing outfit and a training ground to try out new systems and techniques that could be used in the home country. No doubt they stressed rigorous financial controls, cost-effectiveness, and organizational efficiency because many newly acquired companies were in crisis and needed considerable change in the existing organization. The United States did receive some innovations, such as box stores and warehouse clubs introduced by Aldi and the unique home furnishing store designs brought by Habitat.

The Albrecht Group: Introduction of Box Stores

Unlike other acquisitions, Albrecht's entry into the United States in 1976 introduced to this country the concept of no-frill box stores and warehouse stores, which made a profound impact on the retail industry as a whole. That year the group acquired the Benner Tea Company of Iowa and established a subsidiary, Aldi-Benner Inc., which later expanded to 85 stores. In 1979, the group acquired Trader Joe's, a specialty food chain with 18 stores in California, and the following year it bought a minority participation in Albertson's. The group's expansionary moves began to be viewed by U.S. companies as a critical development. Some U.S. companies made counter-moves in the area of limited-range retail stores, among them the midwestern Red Owl chain, Lo-Lo Discount Foods of Gainesville, Florida, Heartland Warehouse Stores in Massachusetts, and Jewel-T Discount Stores in Pennsylvania.

Albrecht's 1980 investment in Albertson's was seen by some as an indication of the expansion programs of Albrecht in the western United States. It was believed that competition between Aldi stores and Jewel-T Discount Stores might be intensified as a result.[16] Although the competition was not increased, warehouse outlets have proliferated in the United States, accounting for an annual turnover of $700 million in 1983.

Membership Warehouse Clubs

The concept of warehouse stores originated in Europe where they originally operated as giant wholesale supermarkets for small food and drug retailers. These stores have been successfully tried in the United States since 1976, at the initiative of Aldi-Benner. Operating as cash-and-carry warehouses, they have expanded their assortment of nonfood items, ranging from appliances to furniture.

During the past few years, more than twenty warehouse outlets have opened in the United States, and several large chains have made plans to get into this line. These outlets began to be known as membership warehouse clubs, with a two-tier membership plan for wholesale and retail customers. The first set of warehouse clubs was founded in California by Sol Price, the founder of the now-liquidated Fed-Mart Corporation. He set up a chain of 12 warehouse clubs, the Price Co., in California and Arizona. In 1983 the annual sales of the Price Co. amounted to $643 million, with a net income of $14.7 million. The concept, based on low margins and high volumes of quality name brand merchandise has spread to other parts of the country, such as the Wholesale Club in Indianapolis and Club Mart of America in New York. Wal-Mart has formulated plans to start warehouse clubs; the Massachusetts-based Zayre corporation has created a new subsidiary, BJ's Wholesale Club, and plans to open two outlets in the greater Boston area in the summer of 1984.

Two key features have made this type of retailing fairly successful: limited membership confined to small business firms and individuals affiliated to large organizations like a credit union and restriction of items to best-sellers in wide variety of categories. By restricting the membership base, the warehouse clubs are able to control several overheads and eliminate losses borne by normal retail stores due to shoplifting and bounced checks. A limit on the categories of merchandise leads to better inventory turnover.[17]

Effect on Employment

The foreign aquisitions have contributed toward maintaining employment by taking over in many cases companies that were either waiting for a successor or were almost in bankruptcy, such as Applebaum Food Markets in Minneapolis and A&P in New Jersey. In several instances, they generated additional employment by launching expansion programs and opening new stores, such as Batus Inc., Dillard Stores, and Food Town.

The foreign-owned companies as a whole employ about 2 percent of the labor force in the United States. Within this small slice, the level of employment rose about 3 percent per year between 1974 and 1977 compared to a 1.6 percent rise in domestic companies during the same period. Within the retail sector, the employment in U.S. affiliates grew most rapidly between 1977 and 1981. It rose from 129,097 in 1977 to 226,756 in 1979 and to 334,383 in 1981.[18]

These trends may be interpreted, though erroneously, as showing that the employment policies of foreign companies are more favorable to workers, and a change in ownership might result in net gains in the level of employment in the U.S. economy. There is no conclusive evidence to suggest that industrial groups from Germany or the Netherlands will adopt any better personnel policies in the United States than what they have been doing back home. And such foreign-based companies, in a desperate bid to turn around a sick company, sometimes have resorted to an indiscriminate closure of retail stores and dismissal of employees. For example, the French management of Korvettes resorted to store closures and employee dismissals soon after assuming control in April 1979 with 50 stores and 9,300 employees in hand. By August 1979, 1,200 employees were dismissed, followed by another 300 in January and 1,300 in February 1980. By June 1980, the management announced that 2,000 more employees would be laid off. By July 1980, all Korvettes stores, other than those within the New York metropolitan area, were closed down.[19]

Such hasty decisions may inflict a great social cost on the host country and even attract public policy interference, especially when the foreign owners do not understand the dynamics of the local environment and the business norms of the U.S. retail trade. The closure of unprofitable stores at various locations may be considered a rational business decision; however, its implementation needs to be carefully phased to avoid any long-term deprivation to consumers of an essential shopping facility. Since foreign acquisitions are likely to grow further in retail industry, the economic and social implications of store closures need to be carefully examined by appropriate state and federal agencies in the United States.

Effect on Retail Productivity

It is not possible to say conclusively whether the foreign acquisitions have increased retail productivity in the United States; however, the managerial policies and programs adopted in many organizations and their financial performance since acquisition indicate some gains in productivity. Although some organizations have continued to suffer major setbacks for quite some time even after acquisition, it is difficult to ascribe such setback exclusively to change in ownership. A number of other organizational and environmental factors are believed to have affected adversely the financial performance of these and some other stores. Many newly acquired chains of grocery, variety, and convenience stores are believed to be doing well. Here too, the hands-off policy of European investors has been effective. Investors have noted the fate of A&P, Korvettes, and Fed Mart, where new management tried to introduce some European formulas and failed, and now prefer to adopt a policy of minimal interference, recognizing the basic marketing strengths most U.S. stores have.

In a few instances, the acquisitions helped such loss-ridden stores as A&P, Gimbel, Spiegel, and F.A.O. Schwartz, which needed a new strategy. The financial results of 1982 and the subsequent quarters of 1983 indicate that A&P is no longer in trouble. The department store operations of British-American Tobacco Industries have been doing well since their acquisition. Although the profits of Saks Fifth Avenue have fallen, all four Gimbels divisions have been operating profitably. The contribution of Marshall Field touched $12 million, and the performance of Saks Fifth Avenue was considered to be reasonable.[20]

Dillard Department Stores have shown an impressive financial performance since Vroom & Dreesmann's investments in 1979. The chain is believed to have installed one of the most sophisticated management information systems available, which has greatly enhanced the administrative capabilities within the orgnization.

The Promodes group of France, which acquired the Red Food chain of stores in 1980, has reported a satisfactory performance of its foreign subsidiaries, particularly the U.S. Red Food stores. The group attributed the 1983 increase in its sales and net profit to the performance of foreign subsidiaries, which contributed as much as 95 million francs in net profit of the total net profit of 164 million francs.

Spiegel seems to have improved since its takeover by Otto Versand. In 1982-1983, the sales of this leading mail-order company rose by 14.3 percent to $485 million. Food Town Stores, a subsidiary of the Belgium group Delhaize Freres, surpassed the nation's leading grocery chains in 1981 in such key areas as return on equity, return on assets, net profit margin, and long-term debt. In the absence of financial rescue by foreign investors, some of these U.S. retail companies may have been wiped out. Thus, the impact of foreign acquisitions on the productivity of the U.S. retail industry on the whole can be considered positive.

The Spill-Over Effect

The impact of foreign acquisitions can be examined from the standpoint of their cumulative long-term effect. Once most foreign-owned enterprises are established and acclimatized, they begin to look for additional opportunities for investment. This leads to follow-up acquisitions in the host country, causing another set of transitional problems, a phenomenon that may be called the spill-over effect. From among several cases of European acquisitions examined in this study, the spill-over effect was especially noted in seven cases, as shown in table 6.2.

Table 6.2
Spill-Over Effect of European Acquisitions of U.S. Retail Firms

European Company	U.S. Subsidiary (if any)	First U.S. Retail Company Acquired	U.S. Retail Firms Acquired Subsequently (Wholly or Partly)
C&A Brenninkmeyer		Ohrbachs (1965)	Maurice, Midwest apparel chain (1978)
Cavenham, U.K. Ltd.	Cavenham (U.S.A.) Ltd.	Grand Union (1973)	Colonial Stores, Atlanta-based supermarket chain (1978)
British-American Tobacco U.K.	Batus Inc.	Kohl Corporation (1972)	J. Weingarten Stores (1981) Gimbels Department Stores & Saks Fifth Avenue, New York (1974)
G. H. Mann (Germany)		Fed Mart, 88% (1975)	Marshall Field, Chicago, 80% (1982) Merged with Vornado Inc., which operates 22 Two Guys Discount Outlets and Builders Emporium, 10 Globe Stores from Walgreen (1978)
Vroom & Dreesmann	Vendamerica Inc., Greenwich, Conn.	Outlet Stores, 15% (R.I.) Dillard Department Stores, Ark. 52% (1979)	H. J. Wilson, catalog showroom, Louisiana, 21.3% Cole National Corporation 14.5% (1979)
Ahold N.V. (Netherlands)		Bi-Lo, South Carolina, 100% (1977)	Cole's acquisition of Child World Inc., 41.5% (1981) Giant Food Stores, Pennsylvania, Maryland and West Virginia, 100%, (1981)
Delhaize Le Lion (Belgium)		Food Town Stores, North Carolina, 51% (1974)	Food Giant (Formerly Altermann Foods), 100% (1980)

In conclusion, the transfer of ownership of U.S. retail companies to foreign hands has had only a small impact on the U.S. economy, although the intensity of impact has been slowly rising. With the limited number of cases at hand and a short history of each case under study, it is difficult to speculate on the long-term trend of financial performance, employment, and gains in retailing know-how and productivity. One positive gain that seems to have come to most of the newly acquired retail companies is the result orientation and the implementation of a disciplined set of policies and processes.

NOTES

1. "A&P Looks Like Tengelmann's Vietnam," *Business Week*, February 1, 1982, p. 42.

2. James Wood, "Golden Touches to Lead," *Time*, November 30, 1981, p. 66.

3. "A&P's Busy Boss," *Business Week*, August 3, 1981, p. 32.

4. "A German Expands in U.S. Retailing," *Business Week,* August 15, 1977, p. 34; Isadore Barmash, "The Invasion of the Corporate Body Snatchers," *New York Times,* February 25, 1979, sec. 2, page 1.

5. Robert Dietrich, "The Rethinking of the Supermarket," *Progressive Grocer*, December, 1982, pp. 49-67.

6. "German Mail Order Firms Eye U.S.," *Wall Street Journal*, March 2, 1982, p. 35.

7. Ibid.

8. *New York Times*, February 25, 1979, sec. 3, p. 1.

9. "Saks Expansion Set; Cost $200 Million," *New York Times*, February 23, 1979; p. D-1; "A Countdown Starts for Gimbels," *Business Week,* April 2, 1979, p. 78.

10. *Batus Annual Reports*, 1981 and 1982.

11. "Batus Retail Operating Net Carves Out 31 percent Gain; Sales Up," *Women's Wear Daily*, April 20, 1984, p. 2.

12. Isadore Barmash, *More Than They Bargained For: The Rise and Fall of Korvettes* (New York: Lebhar-Friedman Books, 1981), p. 224.

13. The Fed Mart Corporation made the decision to close down its retail operation, according to a news brief published in *Wall Street Journal*, April 29, 1982, p. 48.

14. "Merger of 2 Gimbels by Batus," *Women's Wear Daily*, March 22, 1983, pp. 1 and 10.

15. "Batus Changes Wipe Out Field's Retailing Identity," *Advertising Age*, August 2, 1982, p. 36-37E.

16. *International Association of Department Stores, Retail News Letter* (Paris) (February 1980): 15-16.

17. For more details, see "Big Warehouse Outlets Break Traditional Rules of Retailing," *Wall Street Journal*, December 22, 1983, p. 27, and "Warehouse Retailers," *Venture* (December 1983): 107-111.

18. U.S. Department of Commerce, "Selected Data on the Operations of U.S. Affiliates of Foreign Companies," *1978 and 1979 Survey of Current Business* (Washington, D.C., May 1981), pp. 35-52, and (November 1983), p. 20.

19. Ibid., Chapter 15, pp. 243-266.

20. "B.A.T. Says Net Rose 18 Percent in '82; Revenue Up 24 Percent," *Wall Street Journal*, April 8, 1983, p. 32.

7

Foreign Retailing Operations of U.S. Companies

Have U.S. companies gone overseas in search of market opportunities in the field of retailing? If so, what has been the nature and extent of their foreign operations? The vast size of domestic market, it seems, gave little incentive to most U.S. retailers to look for growth prospects elsewhere. Barring the giants like Sears, Roebuck and Woolworth, few U.S. retail companies have ventured to expand into foreign markets. Most that did so went to nearby markets like Canada, Mexico, and the Caribbean Islands.

A number of U.S. manufacturing and service organizations have involved themselves in a variety of retail operations in Europe and other countries for several decades and are still very active. Included are manufacturing companies like Singer, Avon, Consolidated Foods, and Dart Industries (now merged into Dart & Kraft), tire companies such as Firestone, Goodyear, and Goodrich, beauty parlor operators such as Glemby Corporation and Seligman & Latz, oil companies like Mobil and Exxon, travel agents like American Express, and hotel chains like Holiday Inn. The last two decades have also seen a considerable expansion of franchise retail systems in Europe and the Far East, especially in fast-food lines. In this chapter we briefly review the variety of retail operations carried on by U.S. companies in Europe. Statistical information cited with respect to U.S. companies has been taken from their respective annual reports and other material published in recent years.

SEARS, ROEBUCK AND COMPANY

Sears, Roebuck's international expansion dates back to 1942 when its Latin American operations began with the establishment of a retail store in Havana, Cuba. Five years later, Sears opened a store in Mexico City, which marked the beginning of a long sustained chain that now consists of 77 retail stores and 47 sales offices administrated through seven subsidiaries in

12 countries, in addition to interests in Canada.[1] The Sears Cuban Corporation was expropriated by the Castro government in 1960 after it had expanded successfully into eight retail outlets and a central warehouse operation.

Sears entered into two joint ventures in the early 1950s, an Australian joint venture under the name Walton-Sears started in 1955, which was dissolved in 1959, and a Canadian joint venture, Simpson-Sears Ltd., which was formed in 1953 and has continued to operate since then. The latter operates 72 department stores, 4 catalog distribution centers, and 1,263 catalog sales offices in Canada. In June 1983, the parent company, Sears, Roebuck & Co., purchased more equity in this company, raising its voting interest from 50 percent to 60.5 percent.[2]

Sears' entry into Europe took place in 1967 when it opened its first retail store in Barcelona, Spain. The choice of Spain was a natural extension of the experience Sears had accumulated in dealing with Latin American countries having a similar cultural setting. The management visualized good growth opportunities in Spain based on a number of factors such as the presence of a growing middle class, the relatively low investment required, and the high probability of Spain's entry into the European Common Market. Some of these very factors, however, caused problems for Sears' operations there. The cultural similarities between Latin America and Spain led to an erroneous assumption that the two regions had similar economic standards. Management found itself in grave difficulty after its initial decisions on pricing and product mix proved wrong. By 1976, the number of stores had increased to three large and 17 satellite sales offices. Since then, growth has remained rather slow, with no further increase in the number of large stores beyond the two in Barcelona and one in Madrid. Perhaps discouraged by the dampening economic climate and the unrealized hope of Spain's entry into the Common Market, Sears decided in late 1982 to sell the Spanish corporation to a local business.

In 1971, Sears decided to move into Belgium. It planned to acquire Galeries Anspach, an old retail company experiencing financial problems. Sears management hoped to turn around the new acquisition, but mounting costs and an unfavorable attitude of local government and labor unions caused Sears to sell the subsidiary back to the former owners. Sears had difficulty leaving Belgium because stringent local laws and the close tie of small retailers to government and labor unions made it impossible for it to wind up operations unless it agreed to compensate the workers with large sums, equivalent to wages for a three- or four-year period. Finally, the government agreed to allow Sears to sell the operation to the Belgian manager with a pledge to cover his losses for another two years. Thus, Sears was able to get out in late 1976, but it paid for the exit with a $54 million loss.[3]

The operations of the Sears, Roebuck International Division are administered through eight subsidiaries employing over 20,000, ranging in size from a small Peruvian corporation with four selling units to the biggest Mexican subsidiary with more than forty retail outlets. Sears is also involved in the export of management technology to other overseas retailers. In 1976, the company signed a ten-year contract with the Seibu group of retail enterprises in Japan for the export of a total package of retail technology, including management know-how, systems, manuals, and buying specifications.

The international operations of Sears moved in a new direction in 1982 with the setting up of a new subsidiary, Sears World Trade Inc. This unit has undertaken a variety of international activities, including import, export, and other trade support services. It offers management, technological, and financial services to U.S. and foreign firms planning to enter overseas markets. Its main concentration will be the Pacific basin where Sears visualizes a significant potential for growth. Within less than a year, it registered yet another trading company in Japan, Sears World Trade Japan, to engage in the import and export of a broad line of goods and services to finance transactions and handle third nation deals.

F. W. WOOLWORTH COMPANY

F. W. Woolworth Company is considered to be the world's biggest variety chain, popular among the middle and lower classes in the United States, Canada, the United Kingdom, and Germany. Worldwide, F. W. Woolworth Company had 6,927 stores as of January 31, 1982, distributed as follows: Woolworth, 1,707 (includes stores in Canada and Germany); Woolco, 488; J. Brannam, 39; Shirt Closet, 38; Kinney 3,163; Richman, 336; Woolworth-Great Britain 1,132; and Woolworth-Mexico, 24.[4]

The company made its debut in international markets as early as 1907 when it moved to Canada and later opened the first of its British "three and sixes" stores. After a gap of 17 years, Woolworth opened a store in Germany. Woolworth-Great Britain, which was 52.7 percent owned by the parent company, was a leading variety chain in the United Kingdom, Ireland, and the Caribbean. It comprised 995 Woolworth, 13 Woolco, and 18 Shopper World catalog stores. The Canadian subsidiary of Woolworth stretches from the Maritime Provinces to British Columbia and enjoys the distinction of being the second largest general merchandise retailer in Canada, with 209 Woolworth, 100 Woolco discount stores, and ten catalog stores.

Woolworth expanded its operations into Mexico in 1956, operating two stores in Mexico City. In 1957, the expansion continued with the move into Puerto Rico. As of January 31, 1982, there were 24 Woolworth stores in

Mexico, accounting for a sales volume of 2,679 million pesos, 31.9 percent higher than in the preceding year. Woolworth Mexico stores sell general variety store merchandise and apparel and range in size from 20,000 to 40,000 gross square feet. In July 1981, the company sold its share in Woolworth's Mexican subsidiary to Mexican nationals, qualifying under that nation's foreign investment law.

The British subsidiary made many efforts to expand in the late 1970s. It entered the fast-food business under the name Burgermaster. Four foot locker stores were also added. (Foot locker stores are a type of stores in Kinney Shoe Corporation of F. W. Woolworth Company, selling mainly athletic footwear.) The Woolco Catalog Division was expanded. Furnishing centers were opened under the name Furnishing World. The subsidiary acquired a chain of 39 edge-of-town, do-it-yourself retail centers named B&Q (Retail) Limited in 1980. The ground-floor stockroom space in some Woolworth and Woolco stores was converted for do-it-yourself retail use. The store operations were supported by two major data processing centers, a transshipment center network, and two major distribution centers. Notwithstanding these efforts, the subsidiary could not overcome economic slump that overtook Great Britain in 1970s.

The British subsidiary started having problems, as its parent company did in the United States, during the 1970s as shopping habits changed and competition from British retail companies like Mark & Spencer, Great Universal Stores, and British Home Stores began to intensify. Efforts to modify the merchandise mix by getting into specialty items like clothing, furniture, and do-it-yourself goods failed and cost the chain even its core customer group. Losses amounted to $18.37 million between February and July 1982 on sales of $468 million, and its 1981-1982 ROI touched the low figure of 5 percent compared to 23 percent in Mark & Spencer, 20 percent in W. H. Smith, 19 percent in Great Universal Stores, and 13 percent in Boots.[5] In February 1981, a massive price campaign, Operation Crackdown, was launched, but it failed to pull enough people into the stores. Shaken, the parent company decided in late 1982 to sell its entire holdings of the ordinary shares of Woolworth Holding PLC as part of a plan to divest itself of unprofitable properties.[6]

Woolworth's operations in Germany are spread throughout major towns in West Germany with around 200 stores, accounting for an annual sales of approximately $600 million. In the newer stores, the selling area is bigger, and the merchandise has been upgraded to include home improvement items, leisure lines, apparel, and sports equipment. In Germany, too, the company took several measures to offset the impact of the deteriorating economy in the 1970s. It started offering more appealing merchandise assortments and filling the price range between the discounter and the top-level department store in departments like ladies' apparel, sportswear, jewelry, bath soap, drapery, and floor covering. A number of stores now offer quality furs, carpets, and sporting goods for more affluent customers.[7]

SAFEWAY

Safeway's move into international markets dates back to 1929 when it entered Canada. The Canadian operations extend from Victoria to Toronto, with about 290 supermarkets and supporting supply plants. In the early 1960s, Safeway entered the United Kingdom, Germany, and Australia and has since expanded its operations considerably. The three overseas divisions now account for 227 stores, backed by well-equipped distribution centers. Safeway has controlled its environmental diversity by confining its operations in these countries to economically developed and culturally homogeneous regions.

As of the end of 1982, Safeway operated 2,452 stores in the United States, Canada, the United Kingdom, West Germany, and Australia, with annual sales over 17.6 billion. During recent years, Safeway made a move to enter the developing nations by signing a management contract with two large supermarkets in Saudi Arabia and by entering into a joint venture agreement with Casa Ley, S.A. Mexico, a leading West Coast chain based in Culiacán. Safeway bought a 49 percent interest in this chain, which operates eight combination stores, two specialty clothing stores, and three wholesale outlets.

Safeway has recently acquired a 9 percent stake in Allied Import Company, Inc. (Tokyo) in two agreements on foreign trade and information exchange. The Allied Import Company is composed of four Japanese retailers. This new affiliation has enabled Safeway to do a more effective job of handling imported products from the Far East in U.S. and Canadian stores and also to develop overseas export markets for its private labels.

By year-end 1982, Safeway has 535 stores abroad: 294 in Canada, 98 in the United Kingdom, 115 in Australia, and 28 in Germany. The overseas 1981 sales of $4,088 million accounted for roughly 25 percent of total corporate sales.[8]

Lately Safeway has been putting more emphasis on the development of overseas export markets for private labels. Safeway private brands account for 25 percent of the company's domestic sales. In addition to regular exports to Australia and Saudi Arabia, it has been exporting products to Japan and other countries in the Far East.

J. C. PENNEY

J. C. Penney, ranked as the fourth largest U.S. retailer, operates a variety of retail outlets, such as full-line department stores, catalog operations, drugstores, discount stores, and supermarkets. In 1969, the Penney company acquired the Belgian Sarma Company after having held a minority share in it for one year. Sarma-Penney is ranked as the third largest retailer in Belgium and enjoys a good image. As of December 1982, Sarma operated 62 company stores with an average of 29,000 square feet of net selling space devoted to a combination of food, general merchandise, and apparel. The sales in Belgian operations amounted to $565 million in 1982 compared to $748 million in 1981 and $911 million in 1980, affected principally by the stronger U.S. dollar.

Belgian operations also included sales to 188 franchised stores, amounting to $312 million in 1982. Food sales accounted for an average of about 60 percent of Sarma-Penney's sales. In 1971, J. C. Penney established a wholly owned subsidiary in Italy, which operated five stores in the Milan area and sold apparel and household textile lines. This Italian venture was sold to a major local company in 1977. Penney also held a 55 percent share in La Rinascante, Italy's second largest retailer, which it sold in 1980 to invest in catalog selling.

In 1979, J. C. Penney acquired the exclusive rights to develop and operate restaurants under the Wendy system and trademark in Belgium, Luxembourg, France, and the Netherlands. The first of these restaurants opened in Belgium in 1980, but the company closed them in 1982 because of poor operating results. The company did not exercise its option to open restaurants in other countries.

A ten-year program to reposition and expand the Belgian retail operations was announced by the company in 1981. The initial emphasis has been placed on realigning the retail business, traditionally oriented to food and general merchandise, into four segments: department stores, apparel specialty shops, hypermarkets, and franchised food stores.

K MART

In only a few instances have U.S. retail companies acquired established retail companies in foreign countries. Sears, Woolworth, and Safeway made foreign direct investments abroad by creating wholly owned subsidiaries to establish and run their own stores. Among the large retailers, probably Penney is one of the few that acquired a European retail chain. The increasing international involvement of K mart, the second largest U.S. retailer, is worth noting. K mart, operating abroad in Canada and Puerto Rico, recently bought a 44 percent interest in a Mexican retail chain, Astra, a subsidiary of Gentor Group. Astra operates 16 stores in the northeastern region of Mexico.[9] K mart also had a subsidiary in Australia, which was sold to G. J. Coles in 1978. In 1983, it headed in a new direction by starting a trading company, K mart Trading Services, to engage in the import-export business, concentrating primarily on the export of U.S. consumer goods to retailers and wholesalers worldwide.

OTHER RETAIL OPERATIONS

The well-known convenience store company, Southland Corporation, operates 7-11 type convenience stores in Europe and Japan. In 1978 it acquired a majority shareholding in Naroppet, a Swedish group with $12.4 million turnover.

Two other U.S. retail companies made news recently for their acquisition activity on the Continent. In 1979, Searle Optical Group acquired the Brilmij chain of retail eyewear stores in the Netherlands. Searle operated around 460 eyewear stores in the United States, Canada, Mexico, and Puerto Rico at the time of acquisition. The other company was a leading retail jewelry firm, Zale Corporation, which in 1981 acquired 80 percent of a West German group of jewelers, Keller-Christ. This was the first European venture for Zale Corporation, which operated 1,350 retail outlets in the United States and abroad.

RETAIL OPERATIONS OF MANUFACTURING AND SERVICE COMPANIES

Some manufacturing and service organizations are engaged in retailing operations, although the trend seems to be waning. Leading oil and tire companies have established retail outlets owned or franchised in the United Kingdom and other European countries. Esso is believed to have introduced the franchised dealer system in Britain many years back. Similarly, Goodyear and Firestone had retail stores and field distribution centers in many European countries, which later were sold to local companies.

Singer is acclaimed to be the pioneer of chain store retailing in Britain. Its operations were far more extensive in retailing, covering many European countries with a chain of stores, both directly owned and franchised, staffed with well-trained personnel. In 1966, Singer acquired Germany's third largest mail-order firm, Frederick Schwab Company, which at the time had a branch in Italy and a French operation at Reims. The company ran this business for about nine years, selling it in 1975. The continuous decline in the sewing machine market in Europe and rising overheads in the retail distribution system forced the company to reduce gradually the number of company-operated retail facilities in Europe from 1,350 in 1979 to 700 in 1982.

Another manufacturing organization that made a name in building an extensive retail network in Europe and the Far East is the Tandy Corporation, which distributes its consumer electronics products through a chain of Radio Shack outlets consisting of more than 5,500 company-owned retail stores and 3,000 dealer-franchise outlets. The first company-owned stores were opened in Europe in 1974. The number of these outlets gradually increased to 244 in 1978, 319 in 1980, and 491 in 1982, mostly concentrated in five countries; the United Kingdom, Belgium, the Netherlands, West Germany, and France. Tandy has recently entered into a joint venture with the French company Matra to manufacture a U.S.-designed minicomputer TRS-80 model III, which will be distributed by its own marketing network throughtout the EEC region. In 1982, Tandy's overseas markets in Europe, Canada, and the Pacific accounted for sales of $348 million, about 17 percent of total company sales.

Mention may also be made of the gradual rise in the retailing activity of IBM in Europe. With its 1983 revenues reaching $11.5 billion in Europe and a 1987 projection of $16 billion, this company is getting more involved in the Continent. It has created thirty retail outlets and over 1,000 dealerships in this region to provide a strong retail base for its personal computer. The corporation has plans to add another twenty retail outlets in 1984.

Avon Products is well known for its pioneering efforts throughout the world in the field of direct selling. The company is believed to have the world's largest direct selling organization, responsible for selling to customers in their homes through Avon representatives. The company has two main product groups, one consisting of cosmetics, fragrances, and toiletries and the other fashion jewelry and accessories. In Europe, its subsidiaries are located in the United Kingdom, France, West Germany, Belgium, Spain, and Italy.

A few other companies have been active in direct selling in Europe. Fuller Brush and Electrolux, now merged into Consolidated Foods, use a sales force of independent distributors to sell their personal care and household products. Dart Industries (now Dart & Kraft) is also engaged in the direct selling of cosmetics.

Many service organizations have entered this market. The Sheraton group of hotels (controlled by AT&T) and the chains of Holiday Inn and Howard Johnson (now owned by the Imperial Group) are engaged in service retailing. American Express is a global retailer selling a variety of travel and banking services worldwide. Glemby Corporation and Seligman & Latz operate a large number of beauty salons in leased space in major department stores in Europe, especially in England and Germany. Seligman & Latz operated 133 salons and schools in 1982 in Western European countries, out of 208 operated outside the United States, with headquarters in London and an office in West Germany.

The franchise operations of U.S. companies have assumed a much bigger proportion in overseas markets since the early 1970s. Increased competition, exhaustion of prime locations, and an unsettled legal environment in the domestic market drove most U.S. franchisors outside the United States. According to one survey, U.S. franchise companies had established the biggest network of 2,832 units in Canada followed by 2,655 units in Western Europe. Thus, Western Europe has turned out to be a haven for U.S. franchise companies to expand their operations, especially in the soft drink, fast-food, business services, food retailing, automotive services, car rentals, and hotel-motel lines. In the past few years, U.S. franchisors have been expanding more rapidly abroad than at home.

MOTIVATIONS FOR GOING OVERSEAS

Most U.S. companies moved to overseas markets to exploit new market opportunities. To some like Singer and Woolworth, the challenge offered by the overseas markets was as attractive as that offered by the domestic market. These companies sought such opportunities early in their life cycle. Others, like Sears and Safeway, moved cautiously taking up the challenge of international markets gradually to capitalize the strengths they had built in the domestic market.

One of the main motivations for Sears, Roebuck to move overseas was General Arthur Wood's belief that the company should adopt a defensive strategy and expand in areas where there was the least competition. This probably was the reason why Sears skipped the Northeastern region and moved to Latin America. Another important factor was the company's objective to develop multiple pools of capital and people to exploit new growth opportunities.[10]

The large U.S. retailers such as J. C. Penney were also motivated by the opportunity of transferring the mature retailing know-how they had developed. They found that in most countries outside the United States, the distribution function, with its major components of wholesaling and retailing, had remained virtually stagnant for years. The modernization of primary industries such as agriculture, manufacturing, and mining had not been matched by a corresponding modernization in marketing activities. This conspicuous gap attracted many companies overseas.[11]

Another motive was to gain knowledge of markets that might assume greater significance in the not-too-distant future. For example, some U.S companies moved into Spain during the 1970s with the expectation that it would eventually enter the European Common Market and become a more critical market.

Finally, the exhaustion of prime locations and restraints on growth and concentration in domestic markets were important pull factors for many multinationals to explore opportunities outside home. For example, Federal Trade Commission put anti-trust restraints on Winn-Dixie, National Tea, and Federated Department Stores which drove them to other countries for growth opportunities. The same may be true of other companies, including franchisors.[12]

NOTES

1. Sears, Roebuck & Co., *Annual Report, 1981*, p. 14.

2. "Sears to Increase Holding to 60.5 percent in Simpson-Sears," *Wall Street Journal*, June 10, 1983, p. 4.

3. Gordon L. Weil, *Sears, Roebuck, U.S.A.* (New York: Stein and Day, 1977), p. 179.

4. F. W. Woolworth Company, *Annual Report, 1981*, p. 15. In September 1982, Woolworth announced a decision to close down 336 Woolco stores in the United States. *New York Times*, October 5, 1982, p. D17.

5. "The Fraying End of Woolies' Yarn," *Economist,* September 25, 1982, pp. 80-85, and "Woolworth Holdings on Its Marks," *Economist,* September 17, 1983, p. 77.

6. *Wall Street Journal*, December 1, 1982, p. 40.

7. Woolworth Company, *Annual Report*, 1979, p. 12.

8. Safeway, *Annual Report, 1981*, p. 15.

9. "K mart Gets 44 % of Mexican Chain," *Playthings*, September, 1981, p. 12.

10. Sears, Roebuck and Co., *Sears International Story* (Chicago, 1980), p. 1.

11. Thomas J. Bata, address to the Eighth World Conference of Retailing, Toronto, April 19, 1982.

12. Stanley C. Hollander, *Multinational Retailing*, MSU International Business and Economic Studies (East Lansing: Michigan State University, 1970), p. 108.

8

Franchise Retailing in Europe: Role of U.S. Companies

The 1960s and 1970s witnessed a phenomenal growth in the franchise retailing operations of U.S. companies in overseas markets, especially in Canada, the United Kingdom, and the Continent. Franchising has been widely used by U.S. companies as a marketing device to introduce new products and services in distant and culturally diverse markets. It is considered to be an effective mechanism though which a producer or supplier can expand in other countries with minimal risk, overcoming the nationalistic tendencies prevalent in most countries. By giving a franchise, the producer-owner of a new concept (product or service) enables an entrepreneur in the other country to import a know-how and a retailing system that together result in a new enterprise. Each franchise operation creates a self-employed business person and leads to both direct and indirect employment. Furthermore, the creation of a franchise network enables the producer-owner to bypass the conventional channels in other countries and thus retain control on prices, quality, and customer services.

HISTORICAL PERSPECTIVE

The United States is regarded as the home of retail franchises. The Singer Sewing Machine Company pioneered the concept of retail dealership franchises as early as 1863. Singer was followed by other manufacturers, particularly automakers and soft drink manufacturers, which developed franchise operations seen in the 1890s. In 1898, General Motors established its first independent dealer to sell and service automobiles. In 1899, Coca-Cola sold its first franchise in Chattanooga. By the turn of the century, retail franchising had emerged as a principal channel for the marketing of automobiles and petroleum products. Beginning in the early 1920s, several companies dealing in processed food, drugs, hardware, and automotive parts started offering franchises to market their products.

CURRENT STATUS AND INTERNATIONAL GROWTH

Today, after steady growth over one hundred years, the United States is still the world leader in the franchise industry, in both domestic and overseas markets. Franchise-owned retail establishments in the United States claim more than one-third of total retail industry sales. The volume of sales has been growing rapidly. From an estimated $275 billion in 1978, they rose to $289 billion in 1980, to $328 billion in 1981, and to $379 billion in 1982.

Relative to domestic operations, U.S. franchisors have expanded their overseas operations at a much higher rate since the early 1970s. Increased competition, exhaustion of prime locations, and an unsettled legal environment in the domestic market are some of the factors that drove many U.S. franchisors outside the country. According to Department of Commerce statistics, 244 franchising companies operated 14,217 franchised outlets in 1977. By 1982, the corresponding figures had increased to 293 companies and 23,524 outlets, a phenomenal growth (see figure 8.1 and table 8.1).

Another noteworthy trend is the gradual saturation of traditional franchise markets like Canada. Canada's share in the number of foreign franchised outlets fell from 46 percent in 1971 to 31 percent in 1982, whereas concentration has increased significantly in Japan, the United Kingdom, and continental Europe. Singapore, Hong Kong, Australia, and New Zealand are emerging as new markets for U.S. franchise companies, especially those in the fast-food lines.

Earlier research indicated the largest concentration of U.S. franchise systems in three regions: Canada, England, and Japan. South Africa was found to have a large number of U.S. franchise units, a majority of which resulted from the international operations of one drugstore firm. Other geographic regions where U.S. companies had made an impact were Australia, Mexico, and Western Europe. Table 8.2 presents the current status and planned international locations of U.S. franchise systems as of 1975-1976 when Hackett's survey was conducted.[1]

A number of companies that had not set up any foreign operations until the early 1970s either expressed interest or have concrete plans for overseas penetration. Most, however, considered moving into such markets that called for minimal adaptation in the product or service. Adaptation means significant costs and thus has serious implications in any decision to move out of the domestic market. In any case, many companies found no need for any change and were able to extend the same product or service to international markets that originated in the domestic U.S. market.

Currently U.S. franchisors are expanding faster in the foreign markets than at home. McDonald's, for example, has achieved more than 20 percent of its recent growth through overseas business. Many franchise companies

Figure 8.1
International Franchising in 1982

Franchising companies . . . 295
Number of franchising outlets . . . 23,524

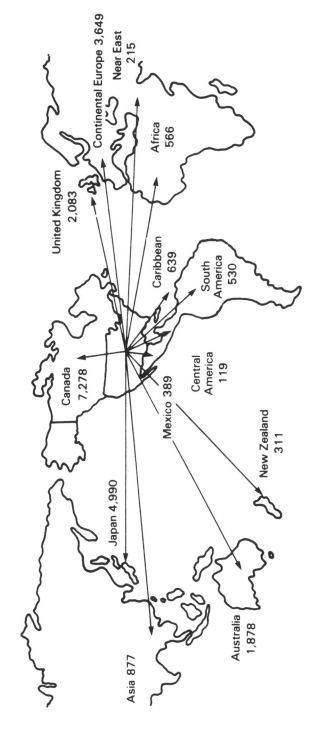

SOURCE: U.S. Department of Commerce, *Franchising in the Economy, 1982-1984* (Washington, D.C.: Government Printing Office, 1984).

Table 8.1
International Franchising, 1982

Kinds of Franchised Business[a]	Location of Establishments									
					Europe			Asia		
	Total	Canada	Mexico	Caribbean	United Kingdom	Other	Australia	Japan	Other	Other[b]
Total, all franchising	23,524	7,278	389	639	2,083	3,649	1,878	4,990	1,092	1,526
Business aids and services	2,421	1,056	21	38	202	421	324	220	46	93
Construction, home improvement, maintenance, and cleaning services	1,410	580	3	24	171	122	30	413	32	35
Restaurants (all types)	4,675	1,172	100	234	481	360	522	1,259	276	271
Hotels, motels, and campgrounds	549	225	28	24	17	160	1	7	44	43
Recreation, entertainment, and travel	160	51	0	5	4	16	29	37	0	18
Rental services (auto-truck)	5,117	707	163	189	356	1,621	360	512	387	822
Laundry and dry-cleaning services	459	362	0	0	11	64	0	0	0	22
Automotive products and services	1,798	854	17	52	129	262	129	131	113	111
Retailing (nonfood)	2,791	1,249	29	37	316	463	382	151	73	91
Educational products and services, rental services (equipment), convenience stores, and miscellaneous	2,872	593	24	7	349	88	100	1,604	98	9
Retailing (food other than convenience stores)	1,272	429	4	29	47	72	1	656	23	11

SOURCE: U.S. Department of Commerce, *Franchising in the Economy*, 1982-1984 (Washington, D.C., Government Printing Office, 1984).

Note: Represents 295 franchisors.

[a]Does not include automobile and truck dealers, gasoline service stations, and soft drink bottlers, for which data were not collected.

[b]Includes South America, 530; Africa, 566; New Zealand, 311; and Central America, 119.

Table 8.2
Present and Planned International Locations of U.S. Franchise Systems

Region or Nation	Operating	Planned[a]
Africa		
South Africa	993	32
Rhodesia	13	5
Nigeria	9	5
Kenya	7	6
Ghana	7	4
Other	32	5
Area total	1,061	57
Caribbean	87	34
Canada	2,832	932
Europe		
England	1,535	259
Italy	255	19
Germany	162	261
France	155	45
Spain	134	32
Scandinavia	101	35
Belgium	90	28
Switzerland	71	19
Austria	42	7
Portugal	35	8
Greece	28	6
Other	47	14
Area total	2,655	733
USSR and Soviet Bloc	8	
Latin and South America		
Mexico	262	148
Central America	87	28
Argentina	62	9
Brazil	51	39
Venezuela	50	10
Other	78	24
Area total	590	258

Table 8.2 (*continued*)

Region or Nation	Operating	Planned[a]
Far East		
Japan	1,087	1,609
Philippines	50	74
Malaysia	41	13
India	19	2
Guam	18	5
Hong Kong	16	8
Other	37	43
Area Total	1,268	1,754
Middle East		
Iran	25	5
Lebanon	22	13
Israel	18	10
Other	65	28
Area total	130	56
Oceania		
Australia	251	205
New Zealand	44	31
Area total	295	236
Total	8,926	4,060

SOURCE: Donald W. Hackett, "The International Expansion of U.S. Franchise Systems: Status and Strategies," *Journal of International Business Studies,* Spring 1976, p. 68. Reproduced with permission.

[a]32 percent of the respondent firms intentionally skipped the planned units column because of uncertain plans or under a claim of proprietary information.

have gradually moved to nontraditional markets such as Kuwait, Morocco, and Singapore.

GROWTH IN EUROPE

In Europe, while there has been noteworthy progress in the direction of large-scale retailing systems, the growth of small and medium-sized convenience retail stores and shopping centers continues unabated in view of rising land values and a rigorous planning of retailing operations in many countries. This is where U.S. companies found a niche. The overseas expansion of these companies through franchises led to the growth of small, independent retailers that had been vulnerable to the growth of hyper-markets and corporate chains.

The environmental factors that induced the growth of the franchise industry in the United States during the 1960s were growing urbanization, female participation in the work force, rising discretionary income, and increasing ownership and usage of automobiles. Similar trends visible in European countries during the 1970s proved to be a gravitating force for the international expansion of U.S. franchisors. To the former vice-president of Hertz International, Mathew L. Lifflander, Europe was the new market of the 1970s in the context of U.S. franchising. According to him, the growing European middle class offered a tremendous opportunity to U.S. franchisors with its rising standards of living, higher income, more automobiles, and increased leisure time.[2]

The franchise systems created by U.S. companies in Europe fell into two broad categories: unit franchise, which implies a single retail business owned or operated by individual entrepreneurs, and regional or master franchise, in which a franchisee is given control over a predetermined region, leaving him free to subcontract the operation to third parties.

A 1982 poll conducted by the International Franchise Association among its member companies revealed that 42 percent of respondents were involved in overseas operations, and an additional 37.8 percent planned to expand internationally in the near future. A large majority, 91.1 percent, used either the master franchising approach offering franchises on a country or regional basis or to individual units directly. The remaining 8.9 percent had taken the route of joint ventures with foreign companies or had established a foreign subsidiary.[3]

The primary reason that drove most U.S. companies out of domestic market was a desire for sustained growth. They had reached a point of saturation in the domestic market, having exhausted all good locations. By the end of the 1960s, the industry was characterized by cut-throat competition. Fast-food franchises had been established in all parts of the country. Thus, the companies started looking for new avenues of growth. Pressures also came from the other end: prospective franchise holders in other countries who showed interest in gaining the rights to develop international territories for mature U.S. franchise systems.

Relative to the overseas operations of U.S. companies, few European franchisors entered the U.S. market. If there was any truly international franchise network with European origin, it was Wienerwalds, the 15-nation restaurant and hotel group headquartered in Munich. From a modest beginning in the 1950s, with first-year sales of $19,000, the organization grew steadily into a chain of 1,508 outlets in 1980—862 in North America and the rest distributed throughout Europe, Japan, the Philippines, and South Africa. Wienerwald's growth in North America provided a major support to its overall expansion. The company had acquired six chains in the United States, including the Miami-based Lums, the International House of Pancakes, Love's Wood Pit Barbecue, the West Coast's Copper Penny Restaurants, and Ranch House Restaurants. The Wienerwald group entered the United States in 1964 through the New York World Fair's, where it operated two Wienerwald restaurants. The real growth started in the early 1970s through application of the franchise concept. On the Continent, 80 percent of the Wienerwald restaurants operated on a franchise basis by 1982. This restaurant chain also conducted courses for their franchisees and field workers each year.

Other foreign franchisors that moved to the United States include Realty World Corporation, Tidy Car, and Grandma Lee's International. Rootes Motors of England had 350 franchised dealers in the United States in 1965. They had sold 250,000 cars in 163 countries in 1964 using the franchise system of distribution. In the fast-food field, the British subsidiary of J. Lyons & Co., Wimpy's, had established franchised units throughout Europe. The acquisition by J. Lyons of the U.S. ice cream chain, Baskin-Robbins, in 1974 further strengthened the international status of this British company.[4]

PROBLEMS IN INTERNATIONAL EXPANSION

The apparent success attained by most U.S. companies in gaining access to international markets should not lead one to conclude that the road was easy. In fact, they encountered a variety of problems that cropped up at every stage: evaluation of target markets, selection of franchisee candidates, location of sites, legal barriers in matters of taxation and protection of patents, and trade marks, maintenance of product quality, and supervision and training of personnel. Operating in a diverse cultural setting made it difficult for the average U.S. company to exercise control on product quality and workers' attitude toward customers. In several instances, the operational methods that proved effective in the United States needed adaptation before they could be transferred to Europe. For example, Pizza Hut faced several unanticipated problems in gaining entry into the West German market. Dining habits of German consumers were found hard to break. The German counterparts had a different perception of managerial duties, refusing to help prepare and serve the food. Labor costs were higher than expected. It was discovered that Germans did not eat pizza with their fingers; they used forks and knives, which had to be supplied to all German units.

Table 8.3 shows that a number of operational problems have been reported, the most common being governmental or legal restrictions. Other problems fall in the areas of personnel management, financing, and marketing adaptation.

A subsequent study undertaken in 1975 found similar problems faced by U.S. franchisors. The fast-food group ranked location and logistical obstacles as the top two problems they faced overseas. Many pointed to high real estate costs as the major problem, especially in Europe and Japan.

Table 8.3
Major Problems Encountered in Establishing
Franchises in Foreign Countries ($N = 52$)

Problems Encountered by Systems	Number of Responses	Percentage
Governmental or legal restrictions	31	60.8
Difficulty of recruiting enough qualified franchisees	23	45.1
Lack of sufficient local financing	19	37.3
Difficulty of controlling franchisees	19	37.3
Difficulty of redesigning the franchise package to make it saleable to franchisees in foreign countries	15	29.4
Trademark and/or copyright obstacles	15	29.4
Difficulty of making the products or service acceptable to foreign consumers	11	21.6
Oppressive tax structure	8	15.7
Insufficient suitable locations	6	11.8
Miscellaneous problems	10	19.6
Total	157	

SOURCE: Bruce J. Walker and Michael J. Etzel, "The Internationalization of U.S. Franchise Systems: Progress and Procedure," *Journal of Marketing*, April, 1973. Reproduced with permission from the American Marketing Association.

The problems pertaining to marketing adaptation did not figure as prominently in this study.[5]

GROWTH OF FRANCHISE OPERATIONS

Some experts hold the view that the United Kingdom would claim to be a pioneer of franchising concept in that English beer brewers, as far back as the 18th century, entered into licensing and financing arrangements with tavern owners for the exclusive sale of various brands of beer and ale. Today some of the well-known British companies using franchise systems include Holland and Barrett, Jet Clean, Spud-U-Like, Kardomah, and Little Chef. The retail sales of the members of British Franchise Association, taken together, have been increasing steadily since 1980, rising by 16 percent to £385 million in 1981 and by 18 percent to £456 million in 1982.

The principal area of franchised growth in the last twenty years has been fast foods. This field has turned into a highly competitive business with both U.S. and British companies. In the nonfood area, many names have become well known, such as Young's Formal Wear and Pronuptia, dealing in bridal wear; Unipart, selling auto parts; Drips, selling plumbing services;

Ziebart, involved in vehicle services; and Service Master Cleaners and TNT Couriers, overnight delivery service operators. TNT Couriers represents one of the fastest-growing franchise operations in the United Kingdom, expanding from ninety franchised operators in 1981 to 257 in January 1983.

Table 8.4 presents data on the growth of the franchise network of U.S. firms in the United Kingdom between 1976 and 1982. The growth during 1980-1982 was slow and even negative in many fields such as restaurants, rental services, auto parts, and educational products and services. It looks as if U.S. companies are reaching a point of saturation in some of these areas.

The results are considerably different when the same analysis is extended to the Continent. The growth seems to be steadily increasing in most fields, as will be noted in table 8.5, although slow or negative growth is found in construction and home improvement, laundry and drycleaning services, and in recreation and entertainment fields. The data contained in tables 8.4 and 8.5 lead to the conclusion that the growth and expansion of U.S. companies

Table 8.4
Growth of Franchise Establishments of U.S. Firms
in the United Kingdom, 1976-1982

Type of Franchised Business[a]	Number of Units			
	1976	1978	1980	1982
Total, all franchising	1,793	1,976	2,031	2,083
Business aids and services	114	118	154	202
Construction, home improvement, maintenance, and cleaning services	208	155	125	171
Restaurants (all types)	433	454	511	481
Hotels, motels, and campgrounds	11	13	13	17
Recreation, entertainment, and travel	22	1	0	4
Rental services (auto truck)	257	280	420	356
Laundry and dry-cleaning services	1	11	0	11
Automotive products and services	256	341	158	129
Retailing (nonfood)	115	170	205	316
Educational products and services, rental services (equipment), convenience stores, and miscellaneous	371	396	410	349
Retailing (food other than convenience stores)	5	37	35	47

SOURCE: U.S. Department of Commerce, Washington D.C., *Franchising in the Economy*, for various years.

[a]Does not include automobile and truck dealers, gasoline service stations, and soft-drink bottlers for which data were not collected.

is much faster on the Continent than in the United Kingdom. It is anticipated that the trend will continue throughout the 1980s.

Table 8.5
Growth of Franchise Establishments of U.S. Firms
in Continental European Countries, 1976-1982

Kind of Business[a]	Number of Units 1976	1978	1980	1982
Rental services (auto, truck)	781	887	1,271	1,621
Businesses aids and services	174	228	332	421
Retailing (nonfood)	134	265	392	463
Construction, home improvement, maintenance, cleaning services	119	234	129	122
Fast-food restaurants (all types)	103	164	249	360
Campgrounds, hotels, motels	59	60	33	160
Laundry and dry-cleaning services	47	50	72	64
Educational products and services rental services (equipment), convenience stores, and miscellaneous	45	59	71	88
Recreation, entertainment, travel	11	12	6	16
Retailing (food other than convenience stores)	10	17	53	72
Automotive products and services	7	169	193	262
Total units	1,490	2,145	2,801	3,649

SOURCE: U.S. Department of Commerce, Washington, D.C.: *Franchising in the Economy,* for various years.

LEADING INTERNATIONAL OPERATORS

It will be useful to look closely at the growth of leading U.S. franchisors in Europe, most of them in the field of fast-food restaurants, which have made tremendous headway in the international market. In fact, more than half of the total number of international units operated by U.S. companies or their affiliates-franchisees in the field of fast-food restaurants are controlled by Kentucky Fried Chicken (KFC) and McDonald's.

McDonald's

McDonald's, the leader in the U.S. fast-food industry and a winner of the American Management Association's 1982 Achievement Award for excellence in marketing programs, was the first company to enter the international market. Although initially its foreign ventures were unprofitable, the company was able to penetrate many parts of the world, thanks to the vision of its founder, Ray Kroc. Kroc's leadership encouraged his company to move into overseas markets even when the domestic market had not been fully exploited. It also helped the company resist an industry trend to higher-priced menus in 1980.[6] McDonald's growth during the 1961-1971 period was high. Annual sales reached $1 billion by 1973. By 1980, sales had jumped to $2.2 billion, 50 percent of which was estimated to have come from international operations. During 1980, the company opened its one-thousandth restaurant in its international division.

The overseas expansion at McDonald's generally took one of the three forms: wholly owned subsidiaries, franchise granted to individuals by the company, wholly owned subsidiary, or affiliate, and affiliates in which McDonald's equity is generally 50 percent or less, with the balance owned by a resident national. In most European countries, the company operates franchised restaurants, though some restaurants are directly operated by the company or its affiliates in England and Germany.

The number of restaurants operated overseas reached 1,341 by 1982. The growth in Europe versus other international regions is shown in table 8.6. Within Western Europe, the growth was mainly evident in Germany and England, as table 8.7 shows.

Table 8.6
McDonald's International Growth, 1978-1982

	1982	1981	1980	1979	1978
Pacific	536	467	414	343	267
Canada	417	389	366	335	293
Western Europe	348	300	245	189	142
Central and South America	40	29	25	23	18
	1,341	1,185	1,050	890	720

SOURCE: McDonald's Corporation, *1982 Annual Report.*

Pizza Hut and Taco Bell

Pizza Hut and Taco Bell are part of Pepsi Company's Food Service Division and enjoy international leadership in their respective segments. Pizza Hut achieved fame throughout the United States as a pioneer of the highly successful pan pizza concept. Pepsi Company Food Service International is responsible for foreign restaurant operations and for food and equipment supply systems at Pizza Hut and Taco Bell restaurants in the United States. This division was represented in 1981 in 18 countries with 237

Table 8.7
McDonald's Growth in Western Europe

	1982	1981	1980	1979	1978
Austria	12	12	7	2	1
Belgium	8	6	4	3	1
Denmark	4	2	0	0	0
England	96	68	51	38	25
France	8	19	17	15	14
Germany	169	155	133	103	81
Ireland	3	3	3	2	1
Netherlands	24	18	17	16	11
Sweden	12	10	9	7	6
Spain	6	1	0	0	0
Switzerland	6	6	4	3	2
Total	348	300	245	189	142

SOURCE: McDonald's Corporation, *1982 Annual Report.*

restaurants, nearly half of which were in Australia. Within a year, the number of restaurants abroad had increased to 284.

The company renegotiated its franchise agreement with franchisees, providing for increased marketing support and more accurately targeted advertising and promotional programs. During 1982, a joint venture was formed in the United Kingdom with a major brewer, Whitbread Co. Ltd., to increase Pizza Hut's potential in this market.[7]

Burger King Corporation

As part of Pillsbury's diversified restaurant group, Burger King is the world's second largest restaurant chain, comprising a massive network of 3,502 franchisees all over the world. System-wide sales of this company reached $2.8 billion in fiscal 1983, registering an 11 percent improvement over sales of the previous year. The 1983 *Annual Report* of Pillsbury Company indicated that the international operations of Burger King "produced substantial operating losses," however.

According to one press report, its recently issued franchise in Switzerland was having problems.[8] In view of that, management was considering transferring basic marketing, franchising, and financial strategies that had worked nationally to the international markets. The company has closed down several unprofitable restaurants to bring its international operations on par with its highly effective domestic operations.

Burger King's long-range plans for Europe provide for the opening of 300 new units by 1987. The company is planning to invest significant additional capital for building new units and refurbishing old ones in Europe.[9]

KFC

KFC Corporation belongs to the family of R. J. Reynolds since Heublein Inc. was acquired by Reynolds in 1981. It operates and franchises one of the largest quick-service restaurant systems in the world in number of units and total sales volume. KFC's franchise agreements grant a license to use trademarks, patents, recipes, and methods of preparing and merchandising specified food products in exchange for a franchise fee. As of December 31, 1982, the company operated in 54 countries outside the United States with 1,386 restaurants. Its major markets include the United Kingdom, Japan, and Australia. In the United Kingdom, it operates sixty restaurants directly and has 300 franchised units.

KFC has recently started penetrating European countries, with its first restaurant in Zurich opened in 1982. The Swiss franchise started as a joint venture and is still endeavoring to make the product concept acceptable in Switzerland. Colonel Sanders' image, which had made a strong impact in the United States, has not been very helpful in international markets. The Swiss partner hired a local advertising agency to build up KFC's image in Switzerland and to fight the conservatism of the local population, who are accustomed to two-hour lunches.[10] KFC's experience in Germany has not been very encouraging either. Some Germans were concerned about the war activities of Colonel Sanders and thought the firm was perhaps a travel agency.[11]

Others

A few other U.S. companies have entered the European market through owned and franchised retail outlets, but relative to McDonald's, Burger King, and KFC, the extent of these operations is limited to a few units. Wendy's, for example, has operations in Switzerland, Germany, Spain, and the United Kingdom, but most are directly controlled. Shakey's Pizza has been expanding in the Pacific and Caribbean regions. Tire companies like Goodyear and Firestone used to have a fairly large-sized retail organization in Europe, but the change in economic and political environment in Europe seen in the 1970s forced them to cut short or sell off operations to local businesses. The same applies to U.S. oil companies like Exxon and Mobil.

CONCLUSION

Statistical information shows rapid expansion of U.S. franchise companies within the European community during the past ten years, a trend likely to continue in the 1980s. The share of franchise operations more than doubled during this period from 2.8 percent to 5.7 percent.[12] Future growth is likely to be selective in the area of contractual franchise chains and will be more pronounced in the nonfood sector.

Experts believe that traditional franchises—product and trade-name franchising and business format franchising—will give way to service franchises, which offer help in a range of areas, including accounting, employment, printing, tax preparation, and real estate brokerage. According to *Nation's Business*, the service sector of franchising grew 7.8 percent between 1978 and 1981, compared to 48 percent growth in the traditional franchise sector. H&R Block, Century 21, and Mr. Build are examples of service franchises.[13]

Though evidence is lacking, it is believed that franchised retail operations have lower failure rates than nonfranchise operations. Advocates of franchise businesses hold that a franchised operation increases marketing efficiency through superior management techniques. According to a British reporter, while 95 percent of small business start-ups fail in the first five years of their operation, the incidence of failure is much less in the case of franchised start-ups.[14]

The degree of success achieved by U.S. franchisors has varied from region to region, depending on the compatibilities of culture and life-style. Many companies found easy entry into Canada, England, and Australia because of such compatibilities. On the other hand, they had problems in continental Europe. Fast-food franchises in general had difficulties in Germany, Switzerland, and France. The Germans, for example, did not easily submit to a strict system of controls and accept an overly detailed contract. The expansion to the Benelux and Scandinavian countries has also been slow, though this mode of distribution is gradually catching on.

NOTES

1. Bruce J. Walker and Michael J. Etzel, "The Internationalization of U.S. Franchise Systems: Progress and Procedures," *Journal of Marketing* (April 1973): 38-46; Donald W. Hackett, "The International Expansion of U.S. Franchise Systems: Status and Strategies," *Journal of International Business Studies*, Spring 1976, pp. 65-75.

2. Mathew L. Lifflander, "It's Getting Popular," *Franchising around the World* 4 (September, 1970): 15.

3. William B. Cherkasky, "Franchising Goes International," *Business America,* November 1, 1982, p. 34.

4. Charles L. Vaughn, *Franchising* (Lexington, Mass.: Lexington Books, D.C. Heath, 1979), p. 193.

5. Hackett, "International Expansion," pp. 72-73.

6. "McDonald's: The Original Recipe Helps It Defy a Downturn," *Business Week*, May 4, 1981, pp. 161-164.

7. Pepsi Company Inc., *Annual Report, 1982*.

8. "KFC Wooing the Swiss Family," *Advertising Age*, January 25, 1982, p. 64.

9. "Burger King Preparing to Open 300 New Units in Europe by 1987," *Restaurant News*, November 21, 1983, p. 18.

10. "KFC Wooing Swiss Family," p. 64.

11. Vaughn, *Franchising*, p. 202.

12. AFRESCO, *Le Movement du Commerce Associé: Chaines Voluntaires, Sociétés Cooperatives de Detaillants*, AFRESCO study 213, Paris, 1973.

13. Nancy A. Rathbun, "The Franchising Wave of the '80s," *Nation's Business*, March, 1982, pp. 82-86.

14. "Franchising: The Low Risk Road to Profit," *The Director*, April, 1983, pp. 46-48.

9

U.S. Retail Industry: Merger Trends and Views on Foreign Acquisitions

The retail industry in the United States has been growing steadily at a compound rate of 8.9 percent, though its growth slowed in the early 1980s as a result of recessionary trends in the U.S. economy. The industry's annual output touched $1 trillion in 1981 and since 1983 has been growing considerably. Food stores, department stores, automotive stores, and eating and drinking establishments represent the major sectors of U.S. retailing (see tables 9.1 and 9.2).

A comparison of 1973 and 1983 reveals that the relative share of eating and drinking establishments in total retail sales registered a significant rise, at the cost of other merchandise categories, except food stores, where one would expect some increase.

Several noteworthy changes are taking place in the character of U.S. retailing, triggered by changing life-styles and environmental challenges. Leading mass merchandisers like Sears, Penney's and K-Mart are shedding some of their traditional hard lines (especially true in the case of J.C. Penney, which recently decided to close down its automotive lines) and moving into nontraditional areas like financial services, real estate, and insurance. These retailers are also getting involved in trading operations in overseas markets, withdrawing from direct involvement in countries like Mexico, Brazil, Spain, the United Kingdom, and Italy. In food retailing, one is struck by the application of computerized systems—the installation of automated teller machines and electronic fund transfer apparatus within the stores. The number of scanning installations has been steadily rising in food stores. It is forecasted that more than 20,000 scanner systems will be in operation by 1987, involving about half of all retail food purchases. Somewhat on the lines of hypermarkets, major retailers have set up superwarehouse stores, stressing low price but at the same time enlarging meat and produce departments, bakery products, restaurant facilities, delicatessens, and take-out foods. Do-it-yourself salad bars, in-store

Table 9.1
U.S. Retail Trade: Trends and Projections
(in Billions of dollars)

	1972	1977	1979	1981	1982	1983	Compound Annual Rate of Growth 1972-1983	Projection for 1984
Retail trade, total sales	449	725	901	1,048	1,076	1,167	8.9	1,266
Employment (000)	11,836	13,808	14,989	15,189	15,122	15,228	2.3	15,335
Sales by major merchandise category								
Food retailing	93	158	199	241	253	262	9.8	N.A.
Department store (general merchandise)	49	76	89	104	107	116	8.1	125
Apparel and accessory stores	24	36	43	50	52	55	7.7	57
Eating and drinking places	36	63	82	99	107	118	11.4	130
Motor vehicle dealers	72	136	141	144	144	175	9.2	194

SOURCE: U.S. Department of Commerce, *1984 U.S. Industrial Outlook* (Washington, D.C.: Government Printing Office, 1984), pp. 48-1 to 48-9.

Table 9.2
Percentage Sales by Major Merchandise Category: A Comparative View, 1973-1983

Category	Percentage of Total Sales Value	
	1973	*1983*
Food stores	21.9	22.5
Department (general merchandise) stores	13.6	12.1
Eating and drinking places	7.9	10.1
Apparel and accessories	5.4	4.7
Automotive dealers	20.3	18.8
Others	30.9	31.8

SOURCE: Ibid., p. 48-2.

bakeries, and fresh seafood departments have become new features in food stores.

The growth of nonstore retailing has been slower than expected because of the continued growth of shopping centers and malls where shopping has been blended with entertainment, social events, and other festivities. The role played by catalog stores and mail-order houses is also on the rise. The development of videotex and teletext systems for in-home shopping has remained rather slow. In the apparel and shoe markets, off-price retailing has been growing rapidly, estimated at about $6 billion, or 6 percent of total sales in this merchandise category. Another significant trend is the emergence of wholesale warehouse clubs in California and Arizona, which sold over $600 million worth of goods at the end of August 1983 fiscal year.

MERGERS AND ACQUISITIONS IN DOMESTIC RETAILING

The trends of mergers and acquisitions are strong in the retailing industry. Offers and negotiations related to the merger-acquisitions of firms in this industry represent an everyday phenomenon. Some are consummated; others drag on for a long time or are ended prematurely. But the pace by which retail companies are changing hands and moving out from one group to another is high and has been accentuated by several factors.

The most important factor in a company's decision to buy rather than build is the need for strategic growth. Retail companies are always looking for promising new entrants to their family to accomplish long-term goals.

The costs and risks associated with the establishment of new businesses are considered high because of the long planning period and the complex dynamics of the retail environment. On the supply side, some corporate groups become unwieldy in size and want to shed one or more of their weaker divisions to enhance managerial effectiveness and financial performance. A need for liquidity to implement modernization and expansion programs is another reason. Not infrequently, tempting offers are made to stockholders, who find them difficult to turn down. In the case of relatively smaller and independently owned companies, the retirement of owner-managers and a lack of suitable successors make it necessary for the organization to find a buyer. Such market nichers, through acquisition by a regional or national company, gain better recognition and get the benefit of fresh managerial support.

Other reasons for merger and acquisition lie in the realm of the changing socioeconomic environment to which a forward-looking company would need to respond by constant portfolio adjustments. Retailers that offered mass market utility merchandise to an erstwhile single-class mass consumption society are now beginning to see the emergence of pluralistic trends—a multiple-segment society that requires strategies of market consolidation and diversification.[1] A&P, Safeway, J. C. Penney, Dayton-Hudson, and many other retail companies had to recognize such undercurrents in the social environment and found adjustment much easier through acquisitions, mergers, and divestments.

Extent of Mergers and Acquisitions

In the 1960s and 1970s, the change of ownership in retail industry through mergers and acquisition was as strong in the domestic market as in the transatlantic. By acquiring existing companies, retail corporations have been able to achieve explosive growth rates. The trend has continued in the 1980s. Discount stores themselves became the target of discount sales in 1980. The number of top discounters was reduced from ten to six in 1980. The biggest transaction was the purchase of Kuhn's-Big K by Wal-Mart for $7.5 million, whereby Wal-Mart acquired all 114 stores in the chain.[2] Surviving discount chains have found acquisition a cheaper means of geographical expansion than the setting up of new stores.

According to the monthly announcements of mergers and acquisitions made by the Conference Board, U.S. retail firms were involved on an average in more than six mergers or acquisitions per month during 1981 and 1982. Within SIC codes 52-59, which cover the main branches of the retail industry, there were 72 cases of mergers or acquisitions in 1981 and 65 in 1982, in which at least one of the involved parties was engaged in some type of retailing. Included among these were leading retailers such as Federated Department Stores, Associated Dry Goods, Melville Corporation, Allied

Stores, Eckerd, Food Town Stores, Limited Inc., Lane Bryant, Ara Services, Zale Corporation, Child World, Kroger Company, Caldor, Hart Schaffner & Marx, and Lucky Stores.

In 1983, the trend continued, with several new companies participating: Southland Corp., Service Merchandise, Gap Stores, and Kohl's Food Stores. The trend is likely to continue and even intensify because of the improved U.S. economic outlook. Carson Pirie Scott indicated in early 1984 that it agreed to buy County Seat Stores, a unit of supervalue stores, for about $71 million. About the same time, K-Mart Corporation agreed to acquire Associated Hosts, a restaurant chain based in California, in an exchange of stock valued at about $80 million. And in April 1984 Limited Inc. attempted to acquire control of the prestigious Carter, Hawley Hale, which sought the support of General Cinema to stave off the unfriendly takeover bid.

Major Types of Retail Acquisitions

Of the hundreds of acquisition that take place in the U.S. retail trade, four broad categories emerge: conglomerate, diversified, vertical, and horizontal acquisitions.[3]

Conglomerates have not been very interested in the acquisition of retail companies, though there are a few examples. Warner Communications purchased the Franklin Mint Corporation, a specialty mail-order firm; Quaker Oats acquired Joseph A. Bank Clothiers; and General Mills acquired the Wild West chain of stores. It is noteworthy that once a conglomerate enters a retailing field, it tends to acquire more retail firms. Both Quaker Oats and General Mills had already gained experience in the retailing field before they made these acquisitions.

In the case of diversified acquisitions, the retail companies are acquired by manufactures (not conglomerates) or other retailers dealing in diverse product lines. The acquired company in this situation is operated as a separate unit or division. Three companies often cited to illustrate the trend of diversified acquisition are Melville, U.S. Shoe, and Limited Inc. Starting as a shoe wholesaler and retailer, Melville entered the apparel field by acquiring a sixteen-store women's apparel chain in 1969. It also entered the health and beauty aids field by acquiring CVS chain the same year. In 1976, it purchased Marshalls Inc. and entered into the field of off-price retailing. Melville's growth continued in the 1980s when it got into specialty retailing through acquiring Kay-Bee Toy & Hobby Shops and Wilson's House of Suede. U.S. Shoe, a footwear manufacturer, entered shoe retailing in 1963 and fields of specialty and off-price retailing by several acquisitions beginning in 1970. The Limited Inc., originally started as a single-unit store in 1967, made rapid strides forward by several acquisitions, especially that of Lane Bryant in 1982.

Vertical acquisitions represent the trend of forward and backward integration, initiated by manufacturers as well as retailers. A major optical manufacturer, Frigitronics, for example, acquired House of Vision in 1982. Sears, Roebuck presents an example of backward integration through its equity interest of a substantial proportion of many manufacturing organizations like Roper corporation and DeSoto Inc. It moved into real estate and financial services in 1981 with its acquisition of Dean Witter Reynolds and Coldwell Banker Co. K-Mart also took a similar direction. In May 1980, it purchased a restaurant business, Furr's Cafeterias, adding Associated Hosts in 1984. Like Sears, it has moved into the insurance line through the purchase of Planned Marketing Association in January, 1974.

Horizontal acquisitions are more prevalent throughout the retailing industry. In these acquisitions, both buyers and sellers are in the retailing field operating at the same level and handling identical or closely related product lines. In such acquisitions, the acquired company is merged horizontally with the existing organization. A number of horizontal acquisitions have taken place recently. Mention may be made of H. J. Wilson Co.'s acquisition of Standard Sales Co. of Florida (July 1981), Wal-Mart's acquisition of Kuhn's Big K (August 1981), Value City's acquisition of Halle's division of Marshall Field & Co. (December 1981), National Convenience Stores' acquisition of 116 convenience stores from McCombs International (February 1982), Best Products' acquisition of Modern Merchandising (September 1982), Heilig-Meyer's acquisition of Thomas Furniture (May 1983), and Joyce Home Furnishings (September 1983), and Kroger Co.'s acquisition of Kroco Inc. (August 1983).

Major Collapses

The years 1979 through 1982 recorded a phenomenal decline in consumer spending in a recessionary environment, which obliged marginally efficient or inefficient retail companies to strengthen their position or file for bankruptcy. In 1982, three major retailers opted for bankruptcy: Wickes Companies, Fed-Mart Corporation, and KDT Industries. F. W. Woolworth shut down its Woolco discount stores during this year. And major food retailers like A&P and Grand Union closed hundreds of their units that were performing badly or were in unsuitable locations.

Mergers and Acquisitions in Franchise Retailing

Franchises are concentrated in fewer hands today than in 1960s. A study made by Urban B. Ozanne and Shelby D. Hunt in 1970 revealed that several franchised systems were acquired by other firms during the period 1966 through 1976. Notable among these acquisitions were those listed in table 9.3.

Table 9.3
Sample of Major Franchise Acquisitions During 1966-1976

Acquired	Purchaser	Year
A&W	United Fruit	1966
Baskin Robbins	United Fruit	1967
Burger Chef	General Foods	1968
Jack in the Box	Ralston Purina	1969
Straw Hat Restaurant, Inc.	Saga Administrative Corp.	1970
Wimpy's International	International Business Assoc.	1970
Dutch Pantry	CPC International	1970
Kentucky Fried Chicken	Heublein	1971
Steak and Ale	Pillsbury Group	1976
Dog 'n' Suds	Frostie Enterprises	1976

SOURCE: Urban B. Ozanne and Shelby D. Hunt, "The Economic Effects of Franchising." Graduate School of Business, University of Wisconsin. Report prepared for the Small Business Administration, Washington, D.C., U.S. Government Printing Office, 1971, A-35. Also, "The Top 400," *Institutions and Volume Feeding* (July 15, 1976), p. 127.

Not all acquisitions lead to good financial performance in the acquired franchise operation. Burger Chef was acquired by General Foods Corporation in 1968 for $16 million. Performance started deteriorating after four years when General Foods announced a pretax loss of $83 million in 1971. In 1967, Burger Chef operated about 700 outlets. By March 1969, the number of outlets had increased to 900; about one-third of these were operated by General Foods directly. By the end of 1970, there were 1,200 outlets in the United States and 36 in Canada. This growth, however, ran parallel to the continued turnover of key executives who started leaving the company shortly after the acquisition. Caught by these unexpected developments, General Foods embarked on a program of pruning the number of hamburger stands, closing down 100 Burger Chef and all 70 of its Rix Hot Roast Beef restaurants.

In March 1982, Hardee's Food Systems, Inc., purchased Burger Chef from General Foods for $43.5 million. Burger Chef had 250 company-owned and 450 franchised restaurants at the time of acquisition. At about the same time, Imasco acquired both Hardee's Food Systems and Burger Chef and announced plans for converting Burger Chef restaurants into Hardee's. Thus, Imasco Ltd., a Canadian conglomerate, became the third largest fast-food franchisor, with 2,074 outlets. Wienerwald's, which acquired Lums and the International House of Pancakes, was trying to sell these operations in 1982 in order to survive.

There has been a noticeable trend of acquisition by larger corporations of otherwise smaller franchise companies, resulting in a concentration of ownership in fewer hands. For example, Pepsi Co. teamed with Taco Bell and Pizza Hut, Royal Crown with Arby's, and Heublein with Kentucky Fried Chicken and Zantigo Mexican American Restaurants. Burger King has teamed up with Woolworth in a move to establish itself in retail stores. Initially Burger King is expected to replace fifty Woolworth lunch counters with its own food units between 1983 and 1988, for a franchise fee, royalties, and a percentage of sales to cover advertising expenses.

HOW DOES THE INDUSTRY LOOK
AT FOREIGN ACQUISITIONS?

Executives from a cross-section of U.S. retail companies operating in the domestic market were approached for their views on the significance and likely impact of this trend. Their observations are presented here.

Significance of Foreign Investments to U.S. Economy

Most industry executives responding seemed either positive or neutral on the issue of rising investments in U.S. retailing. They took a long-term view of the situation and considered foreign investments a generally healthy phenomenon, a reflection of the U.S. economy and a plus for U.S. retailing. As one executive put it, "Capital funds are vital to any economy, and whether they come from foreign or domestic sources, the overall productivity that these funds generate will benefit a lot of people, many of whom are also our customers." Thus, the trend is considered stimulating to the U.S. economy. The investments, many said, come to the rescue of ailing enterprises like "floundering" Gimbels and A&P. In some cases, the foreign investors tried to redeploy the assets of financially weak companies. The French Agache Willot, for example, "finally buried the walking corpse that was Korvette's, converting its real estate to more efficient uses."

One executive took exception to this generally held view, saying that the current trend of foreign investments was unhealthy in the sense that the foreign companies tended to lessen competition, being not as sharp as their U.S. counterparts. In contrast, another executive commented that the investments "many have the effect of strengthening the U.S. economy and maintaining a high level of competition."

One executive looked at the growth of foreign investments as "a natural outgrowth of the development of an international economy: the natural movement of investments to areas offering a greater return on investment opportunity." The investments, in the final analysis, benefited the U.S. economy by preserving or creating job opportunities and by generating tax revenues.

None of the respondent executives favored restriction on foreign investments in the United States. "If they abide by the same rules," one observed, "that apply to U.S. businesses, then there is no need for such restrictions." Such expressions reflected the confidence and optimism of U.S. retail companies in their marketing strategies.

Motivations

What has motivated most foreign investors to put their capital in U.S. retailing? In responding to this question, most executives touched on such factors as the vast potential of the U.S. market, political stability, the work force, easy accessibility, and the desire for diversification. What else could Vroom & Dreesmann do in the Netherlands, one respondent asked, when nothing was left for further growth? According to another executive, foreign investors were seeking a haven for their capital or at least wanted to diversify their earnings base in the event of economic problems in their own countries.

Most respondents believed that foreign investors found far less restrictive business environments in the United States than U.S. retailers faced abroad. Among various foreign restrictions, reference was made to permits required to open or expand stores, difficult and costly labor laws, and requirements for joint management-labor boards among others.

Performance

The trend of foreign investments in retailing is not much different from other segments of the U.S. economy, with the exception that the retail investments have been less successful. Few new techniques have been used by foreign-owned retail companies "with the exception of specialty shops which may be uniquely British."

With some exceptions, the acquisitions saved many marginal operations from going out of business. Many such financially weak operations would hardly attract U.S. investors.

Impact

A majority of industry executives believed that the impact of foreign investments on U.S. retailing has been minimal. The foreign companies in many cases, such as A&P, Korvettes, and Fed Mart, remained preoccupied with the struggle for survival rather than instituting expensive innovation. Most executives considered the foreign companies as passive investors causing neither innovation nor disruption. U.S. retailing will benefit from the introduction of new and productive management techniques brought by foreign companies. All the same, if the results turn out adversely, they would not be held exclusively responsible. The root cause may lie in the already shaky state of affairs in the company at the time of acquisition.

According to one executive, "Aldi, an early example of extremely low cost warehouse and 'box' approach to food merchandising, is one of the few truly innovative approaches that we've seen so far." In some instances, according to other executives, foreign investors injected the needed capital and new management perspectives to firms like Gimbels, A&P, and Ohrbach's "with positive but, as yet, inconclusive results."

One executive observed that the phenomenon was too recent to be evaluated. According to him, decisions to invest in U.S. retailing were strategic business decisions requiring long time spans for benefits to appear.

According to some executives, good innovation ideas traveled anyway, whether foreign investors come to this country or not. Most of the innovations found abroad, such as generics and hypermarkets, had already been tried in the United States by domestic companies on their own, with little success. "Price Club was another example of a firm controlled totally by Americans but successfully based on European mass market techniques." No new ideas have been introduced with a lasting impact. In some cases like those of A&P, Fed Mart, and Spiegel, foreign investments merely prolonged the life of "essentially moribund competitors, without doing anything constructive."

The general impact has been mixed, with some major efforts proving unsuccessful. This is how, one executive commented, "European concepts have been introduced before adequate understanding of the U.S. consumer."

The Future

Will the current wave last? A majority of respondents believe that the trend will continue, though they do not expect it will accelerate. Explaining reasons for the anticipated slow move, the executives said that not many retailers abroad had the resources to operate in the U.S. market. Some investments have led to disappointing results. Moreover, the appreciating dollar may slow down, if not reverse, the present momentum.

NOTES

1. Jagdish N. Sheth, "Emerging Trends for the Retailing Industry," *Journal of Retailing* 59 (Fall 1983): 14.

2. "Discounters Buy Rather than Build," *Chain Store Age Executive* (July 1982): 28.

3. For a good survey of recent retail mergers, see Gilbert W. Harrison, "Retailer Mergers," *Mergers and Acquisition* (Winter 1983): 40-50.

10

Concluding Observations

Retailing operations of U.S. companies in Europe have been waning in recent years. The national mass merchandisers—Sears, Woolworth, and J. C. Penney—have not found their European operations as challenging as they had anticipated prior to entry, for two reasons. First, the political-legal environment in some countries proved hostile or not as cooperative as they had expected; second, the hope that member nations of the EEC eventually would agree on one major policy regarding regulation has not been realized. These major retailers and some others have gradually decided to withdraw. Sometimes they were at fault. Sears, for example, failed to judge accurately the potential of the Spanish market. And Woolworth was unable to keep pace with Britain's quickly changing retailing environment and consumer profile.

U.S. companies seem to have become more active in the service sector, especially in fast-food retailing in Europe and other parts of the world. And recently, leading retailers like Sears, K mart, and Safeway have moved into international trading operations, especially in the Pacific region.

Perhaps this background explains the indifference of the domestic retail industry toward direct investments from Europe, an important transatlantic phenomenon. The industry does not seem to be much concerned about it, mainly because the magnitude of the intrusion is still proportionally small. In fact, retail firms in general have welcomed the investments, as have the investment bankers and financial brokerage firms who profited from their involvement in these transactions.

The size of investments in the trade sector has been rising. It has jumped from $15 billion in 1980 to $25 billion in 1983. The share of retail trade has risen consistently during this period; however, it has not yet reached a point that should cause alarm to government or industry.

Foreign investors control more than 24 major retail and food service chains with a combined sales approximating $30 billion. Of special significance is the inroad made by these investors in food retailing. A continuation of this trend might put 25 percent of the U.S. food retail business in the hands of foreign companies by the end of the 1980s. But even in this situation, a 25 percent control over food retailing amounts to barely 10 percent control over the total U.S. retail business. In the rapidly growing trillion-dollar U.S. retail industry, even this extent of foreign participation should not be considered excessive or counterproductive, though the domestic industry has shown some concern. One reflection of industry's concern has been noted in newspaper advertisements. A full-page Winn Dixie advertisement, for example, included statements emphasizing American ownership.[1]

Foreign investments have given a new lease on life to many retail companies that otherwise would have gone out of business. No doubt in a few cases, foreign investors faced difficulties, particularly when they decided to transplant some European ideas to the U.S. stores. The unsuccessful efforts made by the new owners of A&P and Fed Mart to apply the European experience made it abundantly clear that the U.S. retail industry has reached a point of maturity and sophistication; it would not accept a new technique just because it was successful abroad. The lesson learned by most investors can be stated as follows: Exploit the opportunity but do not go too far. Remain an investor. Keep a low profile. Do not meddle with the local environment.

The U.S. retailing industry seems to have benefited from these investments. Many retail companies were starving for new capital to support growth programs, to open new stores, or to renovate old ones. Their stores needed a better layout, a more appealing interior, and a merchandise mix that would match new life-styles. With dramatic changes in market profile, the stores needed more effective locations and more dependable logistics support. All of this required funds, but domestic investors were not excited about funneling more money into retailing. Thus, this gap was filled by foreign business firms. Domestic retail firms welcomed it because it ensured the revival of ailing or inefficient stores, enhanced the competitive environment, gave new business to other sectors, and thus boosted the U.S. economy.

Besides lack of capital, the domestic retail industry had also suffered from poor management, outdated methods and procedures, and a feeling of indifference or complacency toward the marketplace. No doubt, the U.S. economy witnessed an impressive technological growth and managerial sophistication during the 1950s and 1960s, but the impact of these developments was hardly visible on the retailing industry. Most retail companies followed outdated practices and had failed to recognize the undercurrents of a highly dynamic marketplace.

The cases presented in this book, as well as the views expressed by U.S. executives, made it clear that the involvement of European companies in the

United States is hardly an invasion of the U.S. retail industry. In most cases, the objective of the European investors seemed to be a profitable investment with minimal interference in day-to-day operations in the acquired company. There is no evidence whatsoever of a plan to dominate the retailing sector of the U.S. economy.

Is the U.S. retail industry for sale? There are no serious legal barriers in the United States that restrict the acquistion of retail companies or, for that matter, companies in other industries by foreign investors. With few exceptions (in sensitive areas like banking and defense), foreign investments are treated and regulated almost in the same way as domestic investments. In the wake of such a liberal economic and legal environment, the trend of foreign investments is likely to accelerate, especially when it finds support from exogenous factors such as a favorable fluctuation in stock prices, exchange rates, or interest rates.

Encouraged by some favorable environmental developments, foreigners have been investing in the United States over a great many years. The present wave of acquisitions in the retailing sector is a continuation of this situation. Despite its huge structure and a steady growth rate, the U.S. retailing industry remained for a long time a neglected sector in the U.S. economy. Even large retail corporations like A&P, Montgomery Wards, Grand Union, and Gimbels suffered setbacks for taking a myopic business approach. The foreign investors saw certain basic strengths in the U.S. retailing business. They found it to be relatively stable and less vulnerable to recession. They got interested in buying basically sound companies which may not be financially top-notch but had certain inherent strengths like good location and an attractive net worth.

Although the primary motivation among most European companies has been to secure a good investment, some took the initiative in streamlining the organization of the acquired company. In fact, many had to make strategic decisions in order to put the new affiliate back on the right track. The post-acquisition period witnessed a number of managerial changes in some companies. Organizational structures were realigned. Management information systems were installed. Changes were introduced in the merchandise mix in response to new life-styles. Locations were reexamined from the standpoint of long-range growth plans. Top management provided necessary support to establish programs for personnel training and development. Some companies learned, probably for the first time, how to operate under environmental pressures or respond to crisis situations, as their European parents were used to.

Does this mean that instead of being a net exporter of marketing know-how, the United States has become a net importer of such retailing know-how? It is difficult to generalize, but clearly some of the acquired companies needed help from the outside, among them, Grand Union, A&P F.A.O. Schwartz, and Bi-Lo. Some evidence suggests that improved organizational and managerial systems were introduced in many companies in the post-acquisition period. In most cases, the new techniques and systems were basically American, but they came to the rescue of these companies at the initiative of European investors, resulting in a two-way flow of retailing know-how: a know-how that had originated in the United States but came to rescue the U.S. retail companies via Europe.

This flow took several routes. Many executives-owners of European retail companies, especially the younger ones, had attended U.S. business schools or acquired experience in U.S. stores. New ideas were disseminated through professional meetings held by the National Retail Merchants Association, the International Franchise Association, and the Food Marketing Institute. Many burgeoning retail companies in Europe invited U.S. consultants during the 1960s and 1970s to get help in planning new investments in their organizations to support programs related to store layout, interior design, merchandise mix, and product display. This period also witnessed a significant shift in the orientation of business education in European institutions of higher learning, moving away from traditional schools of commerce to more case-oriented programs with an eclectic approach patterned after the curriculum in U.S. business schools. This change in orientation gave greater opportunities and incentives to U.S. business professors to visit schools in the United Kingdom and on the Continent for teaching, research, and consulting. In the process, many European executives, including those from large retail companies, came in close contact with the marketing and retailing professors from the United States.

Foreign investments are not detrimental to the growth of individual U.S. retail companies or the retail industry as a whole. Indeed they brought about a sense of discipline and a new orientation in planning in many companies that were the recipients of such investments. If the flow of foreign capital contributed to higher productivity and growth, the U.S. economy has gained. Consumer interests have been better served, employee job prospects have become brighter, and the industry as a whole has received a boost. Even the threat of acquisition has resulted in some constructive thinking on the part of top management in streamlining the organization. For example, Brescan's bid to take over Woolworth in April 1979 made Woolworth's top management realize that it needed to be a more diversified and aggressive company if it wanted to live beyond the century it had just completed.

What might be considered a critical factor is not the desirability of a fresh approach but the process followed in implementing it. A retail outlet, especially for consumer goods, is an essential marketing facility; it should not only make a profit but also serve the community's day-to-day needs. Thus, the profit goals of a retail enterprise need to be carefully intertwined with community service goals in the process of formulating strategies. Post-acquisition changes in some companies, however, failed to reflect this societal orientation. After Agache Willot took over Korvettes, there was an indiscriminate closure of several stores within a short period of time, rendering thousands of employees jobless. Similarly, the reorganization programs at A&P and Grand Union resulted in the closing of hundreds of retail outlets. The communities that had been shopping at these outlets for years were deprived suddenly. The same could be true of Fed Mart stores in California, Colonial stores in Georgia and Outlet stores in Rhode Island.

Foreign investments in the U.S. retailing business are likely to increase in the future. Even recent gains in the dollar did not have a dampening effect on this trend from 1980 on. The economic and political environment in Europe is likely to remain turbulent and unstable. On the political front particularly, the East-West gap is not likely to be patched in the near future, despite the rising volume of Soviet trade with West European countries. Thus, leading business firms in Western Europe, having faith in the free enterprise system, will continue to look to the United States for opportunities. Encouraged by their initial investments, many European investors have sought additional acquisition deals with U.S. retail companies. In April 1984, Albertson's, a leading U.S. supermarket chain, announced that its 1980 agreement with Theo Albrecht stiftung has been amended to allow Albrecht to raise its holding from 9.9 percent to 12 percent in Albertson's. Because this trend is likely to continue, it is all the more desirable for U.S. regulatory bodies to evolve guidelines for closure of stores, dismissal of employees, and the spill-over effect.
stores, dismissal of employees, and the spill-over effect.

The story of European investments in U.S. retailing is thus one of impressive performance and frustrating failures. The same could be said of acquisitions of retail companies in the domestic sector. It would be useful if the foreign investment cases are examined closely to identify the causal factors in the success or failure. An identification of these factors might enable prospective investors to ensure a smooth change of hands and a productive transfer of retailing know-how that occurs in the process. The discussions I had with members of the trade in the United States and Europe, as well as a follow-up of published data on the organizations studied, revealed the following:

1. An effective transfer of ownership and know-how occurred in those branches of the retail industry that had a well-developed operating system or formula, sufficiently tested in other countries, such as a price club, a mail-order house, or a home furnishing specialty shop. In other types of retail businesses, such as grocery chains and department stores, the experience of European investors was hardly an advantage. In such a sensitive area as grocery retailing, when the new owners tried to transplant their innovations, the results were disappointing. The attempts to convert Fed Mart stores into hypermarkets did not work. Similarly, conversion of some A&P stores to Plus stores was not satisfactorily achieved. But many

acquisitions of specialty chains and mail-order houses showed satisfactory results. For example, Franz Carl Weber's acquisition of F.A.O. Schwartz, Otto's acquisition of Spiegel, and J. Lyons' acquisition of Baskin Robbins did not evidence many problems in the transition phase.

2. Acquisitions have been more successful in selected branches of retailing like convenience stores, especially in the sunbelt states, which have experienced significant growth in the last two decades. Thus, the probability of success seems higher in the sunbelt region, which is less vulnerable to economic recession and climatic upheavals.

Attempts to recreate hypermarkets or their prototypes have not succeeded, for several possible reasons. One is a buyer psychology or a shopping behavior pattern that is not used to buying hard goods along with groceries, clothing, and housewares. Second, the multiplicity of outlets functioning in U.S. retail markets—department stores, variety stores, discount department stores, convenience stores, drugstores, self-service supermarkets—makes it difficult for hypermarkets or superstores to carve a niche in the U.S. retail market. Third, the liberal legal environment in the United States provides no insulation for the exclusive operation of a hypermarket within a given trading area as in Europe. The hypermarket concept worked well in Europe because the retailing industry there had remained relatively stagnant for quite some time, leaving a large gap to be covered by some innovative retail institution. The emergence of hypermarkets filled this gap. Moreover, hypermarkets are protected by law; no other similar store is allowed to operate in the same trading area. This enabled them to get patronage from a cross-section of ethnic groups and nationalities living at times in two or more countries.

3. A policy of distant surveillance, minimal interference, and a low profile has worked effectively in successful acquisitions. The need for such an approach has restrained most investors from proclaiming foreign ownership by setting up their own stores or service centers. This policy reflected a respect for and an understanding of cultural disparities. As a seasoned retailing executive rightly said, "The greatest danger in international retailing is a certain ethnocentrism. Unwittingly and subconsiously one always expects people in other countries to have the same standards in life, to behave, to act and to react the same way as the people back home. Some sensitivity and humility is needed to look and listen instead of talking and to start one's learning curve about alien peoples and cultures."[2] Even moving next door within Europe, in some instances, proved a fatal venture, let alone moving to the other side of the Atlantic. Karstadt, for example, had problems in operating a quiet joint venture in France, with Swiss collaboration. Carrefour could not penetrate effectively in West Germany and some retail companies from the Netherlands faced serious problems when they wanted to expand into Belgium.

In conclusion, it may be observed that a serious attempt to turn around a sinking organization is one thing, but an acquisition propelled by short-run hopes of making money quickly is quite another. The closing of a few hundred unproductive A&P stores might be considered a worthwhile social cost if the action ensures the survival of the organization as a whole. But foreign investors should not be able to play with the fate of workers, consumers, suppliers, and financiers in the United States. I believe that a suitable regulatory process needs to be established in the United States, as it is already in some European countries and Canada, under which it is possible to ensure that acquisitions do not result in social and economic disruptions and that essential retail facilities are not exploited.

Much has occurred in retailing on both sides of the Atlantic. Many trends have appeared in the past two decades. First is a marked flow of retail technology to and fro. The techniques of self-service, discounting, information and control systems, shopping center development, and franchising have flowed to Western Europe and were adopted there. The United States has also been the recipient of some ideas, among them the concepts of box store retailing and hypermarkets. Second, the 1970s and 1980s witnessed a trend of foreign direct investment in retailing by many European investors. The trend of direct investments from the United States has remained comparatively weaker. U.S. retailers have not found the European environment favorable to their style of retailing. Many, under the constraints of the political and legal environment, opted for other avenues of international involvement, such as service retailing, fast-food franchises, or otherwise export-import trading. They have also entered into management contracts to help the development and modernization of retailing. The last type of involvement is especially marked in the Pacific region. It is believed that many leading U.S. and European retail companies will play a greater collaborative role in Africa, the Middle East, and the Far East in the future. The role of large retailers in stepping up the economic growth of developing nations has remained a significant feature of international retailing, though it has often gone unrecognized. Not many remember how much Sears, Roebuck did for several Latin American countries. Similarly, few realize the magnitude of growth support provided to developing countries through the buying operations of leading retail companies in the Pacific region. Clearly international retailing will be a far more challenging area of international business in the next two decades than in the past.

NOTES

1. *Seneca Journal-Tugaloo Tribune*, Seneca, S.C., December 8, 1982, p. 7-B.
2. Speech delivered by Dr. A.C.R. Dreesmann at the Seventh World Conference of Retailers, Tokyo, June, 1980.

APPENDIX A

Some Comments on International Retailing

The largest expatriate retailer in the world is probably the U.S. Army-U.S. Air Force Exchange Service. That statement does not contradict, in fact reinforces, three generalizations about expatriate retailing: (1) expatriate retailing is not a new phenomenon; (2) expatriate retailing is very often merchandise based; and (3) expatriate retailing encounters varying degrees of welcome and resistance.

Retail merchants have operated outside their own countries for many years, even many centuries. Putting aside all questions of itinerant peddlers, merchant caravans, and the like and putting aside all questions of the extent to which trade in various parts of the world is in the hands of resident aliens, we can still find many historic examples of stores in one country having been operated by organizations domiciled in other countries. The largest contemporary Canadian retailer, the Bay, was headquartered in Britain until a relatively few years ago. Interestingly enough, two of the leading Argentine department stores, Harrods and Gath, established fairly early in this century, were also of British origin. Certainly most U.S. department and specialty stores that adopted such names as "the Paris Store" were not French owned, but there was some substantial French investment in Latin American, particularly Mexican, retailing. More substantially, British, French, Dutch, Swiss, Belgian, German, and Australian trading companies that were interested in African, South Pacific, Asian, and South American raw materials cultivation and extraction became involved in storekeeping.

I am curious about, and am working on, the extent of U.S. investment in foreign retailing and foreign investment in U.S. stores in the 1920s and 1930s. Certainly numerous "snob" high-status firms tried to cultivate a cosmopolitan "Paris-London-New York" image at that time. Some of this was a charade—an overseas mail box or a little desk space in a resident office masquerading as an international operation. But other instances consisted of true cross-border branches. We know that some U.S. chains, such as Woolworth, established foreign offshoots. European participation in U.S. mass merchandising must have been either limited or very discrete. The vigorous anti-chain lobby always protested the entry of New York, Wall Street money into local retail arenas. I imagine that it would have welcomed an opportunity to attack foreigners, yet it does not seem to have used that theme. Yet I seem to recall bits and pieces about foreign investment in pre-World War II U.S. trade and am pursuing that trail.

The military exchange service is well run, but its attractions lie mainly on the merchandise-price axis rather than the retail ambience-service axis. Many of the trading company retailing efforts started as commissaries for their expatriate supervisors (some began by introducing goods to trade for local raw materials). Other expatriate stores were founded to cater to travelers and fellow citizens residing abroad who wanted a "home away from home." The old home newspapers, magazines, foods, spirits, pharmaceuticals, and gadgets were, and are, the drawing cards.

The luxury stores, the couturier shops, and the fine jewelers, who receive so much of our attention and do such a small percentage of the retail trade, may attract customers in part by their style, distinctiveness, and merchandise presentation. But supposedly Gucci, Pucci, and all the rest turn out a superior product.

Closely related to the snob shops are the demonstration outlets, maintained by some foreign manufacturers to show "how it should be done, and "what can be done." They may introduce new visual merchandising tactics, but those tactics simply underlie the merchandise.

Some manufacturers have gone further and set up vertically integrated channels. These are almost always product driven. There are other, nonproduct, bases for retail investment abroad. There are instances, successful and unsuccessful, of exporting retailing techniques. Some of us with long memories can recall the time fifteen or twenty years ago when the world was to be covered by replicas of Le Drug Store, a French fantasy of U.S. pharmacies cum soda fountain. This dream proved ephemeral, but there have been more profitable international transfers of department store, mail order, supermarket, and superstore technology.

Much international participation in domestic retailing is purely financial. Varying exchange rates, varying levels of national prosperity, varying degrees of retail saturation in different countries, and various levels of nervousness about future social, economic, and political conditions influence the flight of retail capital. Many of Europe's largest retail firms are owned or dominated by families that can remember generations of domestic turmoil. I suspect that their instinct for risk diversification expressed itself in American investment in the 1970s because of both their own prosperity and the favorable position of their currencies at that time. *Chain Store Age* recently pointed out that foreign firms pay no U.S., and often no homeland, capital gains tax on profits from the sale of retail locations. That presumably helped them outbid U.S. investors for the acquisition of chains with valuable properties. The French acquisition of Korvettes may have been influenced by this advantage. Foreign financial participants often remain fairly far aloof from the actual operations of the stores they have acquired. This may often be a wise decision in view of the difficulty of learning the nuances of merchandising, site selections, promotion, and personnel administration in another country.

Finally international retailers are sometimes warmly welcomed and sometimes hotly detested. Retailing is so public in nature that it can easily evoke chauvinistic reactions. When General de Gaulle decided that France needed supermarkets and French-Canadians were honorary French nationals, Steinbergs of Montreal was a welcome entrant into French trade. Steinberg's French subsidiary, Supermarches Quebec, emphasized their Canadian flavor with totem poles, pine trees, and smoked salmon. Then the official attitude changed, and Supermarches Quebec learned that it should appear somewhat more Gallic. There are numerous other examples, but one point emerges: we may be able to distinguish the international snob shops from the international mass retailers on the basis of whether they proclaim or hide their foreign ownership.

Stanley C. Hollander

Multinational Retailing: Are the Food Chains Different?

Multinational retailing—that is, retail firms operating in more than one country—has a long history, both in America and Europe. The history has also been a checkered one, in that there have been periods of grandiose expansion and periods of hurried withdrawals.

The specific retail trades in which multinational retailing has developed in the past have been many and varied. The high-class luxury goods trades is one case, with firms like Van Cleef and Arpels or Harrods becoming multinational at least for a while. There have been the retail outlets in many countries linked with manufacturers, such as the Singer sewing machine company in the nineteenth century and the Bata footwear shops in the twentieth. There have been the mass merchandisers such as the U.S. F. W. Woolworth (in the United Kingdom in 1909, in Germany in 1926, and in Spain in 1966). And in the food trades, two striking examples, from a number, are the German firm L. Gottlieb, which had some 300 branches in France before World War I, and J. Meinl of Austria, which had some 3,000 branches in five different countries before World War II.

World War II brought to an end many of the multinational experiments, but after a period of quiescence, and above all in Europe with the development of the Common Market, interest has revived strongly. The list of retail firms that are operating or planning to operate on a multinational scale is growing yearly.

But a feature of this recent upsurge in multinational retailing activity has been the strong emphasis in the nonfood sector and the relative absence of activity in the food sector. (This contrast certainly does not apply to the food manufacturing and processing industries, where multinational actions have been very numerous in the last few years. But this discussion is confined to retailing.)

Without covering all the countries in the world or using a long time span, the contrast between the multinational retailing activity in the nonfood and in the food trades can be illustrated by restricting the examples to the countries of the enlarged Common Market and to the actions that have been taken or planned in the last three or four years.

Reproduced with permission from "Comité International des Entreprises à Succursales," Paris, no. 8, 3rd quarterly, 1973.

In the nonfood trades recent multinational retailing activities have been as follows. This list is confined to recent actions and to the Common Market countries. Many of the firms listed have already established multinational links in earlier years and in other countries—for example, Great Universal Stores in the Netherlands, Sweden, and Austria; C&A Brenninkmeyer in the United Kingdom, Belgium, and Germany; Quelle in Austria and Luxembourg; Sears in Spain and Mexico; Prisunic in Greece and Spain.

Name and Country of Multinational Firm	Trade	Country of Expansion and, Where Applicable, Name of Linked Firm
Great Universal Stores (U.K.)	General retailing and mail order	100,000 Chemises (France)
Sears Roebuck (U.S.A.)	Department stores	Galeries Anspach (Belgium)
J. C. Penney (U.S.A.)	Variety stores	Sarma (Belgium) Italy
Quelle (Germany)	Mail order, photo	France
Neckermann (Germany)	Mail order	Netherlands
C&A Brenninkmeyer (Netherlands)	Textile retailing	France
Dixons (U.K.)	Photographic goods	Rinck (Netherlands)
La Redoute (France)	Mail order	Sartha (Belgium) Vestro (Italy)
House of Fraser (U.K.)	Department stores	Illums (Denmark) Switzer (Ireland)
André (France)	Footwear retailing	Shuh-Jansen (Germany)
British Shoe Corporation (U.K.)	Footwear retailing	Hoogenbosch (Netherlands)
Mothercare (U.K.)	Children's wear	Denmark, Germany and the Netherlands
Prénatal (France)	Children's wear	Italy
Combined English Stores (U.K.)	Textile retailing	Lindor (Belgium)
Richard Shops (U.K.)	Textile retailing	France
Austin Reed (U.K.)	Men's wear retailing	Netherlands and Ireland
Prisunic (France)	Variety stores	Germany (Saar)
K Shoes (U.K.)	Footwear retailing	Hessels (Netherlands)
Marks & Spencer (U.K.)	Variety stores	Belgium and France (planned)
Roche-Bobois (France)	Furniture	Belgium

An earlier, well-publicized example is Burton (U.K.) in France and Belgium.

In the food retailing sector, the cases of recent multinational activity, using the same definitions, are limited to:

Carrefour (France)	Belgium, Italy, and UK (minority interest)
Matthews Holdings (UK)	Boucheries Bernard (France)
Albrecht (Germany)	Combi (Netherlands)
SHV (de Gruyter Marko) (Netherlands)	Frowein and Nolden (Germany)

Earlier multinational moves in the food trades that can be listed, are Safeway (United States) operating in the United Kingdom and Germany, Weston (Canada) operating in the United Kingdom, Germany, and France, and, until recently, Steinbergs (Canada) operating in France.

Faced with these two lists, the question can be asked, Is the food retailing sector different in respect of multinational operations? Some argue that the food sector is different. There are important variations in consumer taste in different geographical areas, and these, it is suggested, limit the advantages of multinational operations in the food trade, the implication being that differences in consumer tastes in the nonfood sector are less marked. The variations in consumer taste for foodstuffs in Europe cannot be denied, but on the other hand, food manufacturers operate on a European scale in many instances, and, furthermore, some adaptation of the assortment to local taste is a normal practice in food retailing (as it is also the practice in nonfood retailing).

A second argument, that food is different, develops the theme that the economies of scale of buying on a multinational level are less evident in the food than in the nonfood sector. (This, of course, links up with the argument about differences in taste.) But here the importance of joint buying on behalf of multinational retail firms in the nonfood sector should not be exaggerated. They draw heavily, in most cases, on local supply markets, except for merchandise imported from another hemisphere, which, of course, is what happens in the case of the international voluntary wholesale chains, like Spar, in the food trades.

A third argument, a bit more complicated, is that while the marketing policies of nonfood retailers are usually aimed at a particular sector of the market (income sector, age sector, urban or rural sector, etc.), the food retailers usually aim at a very wide sector of the market. The market target of a multinational retailer in the nonfood sector is, therefore, much more precise (and perhaps attainable) than in the food sector. This argument has a ring of truth except, of course, for those food retailers who do have a specific market—for example, a very restricted assortment with discount prices (Albrecht in the Netherlands or Denner of Switzerland in Austria).

But the basic reason for the present contrast between the extent of multinational retailing in the food trades and in the nonfood trades in Europe would appear to lie not so much with the technical arguments advanced above as with the particular historical situation of the European food retailing industry in the 1960s and early 1970s.

The factors that have led, and are leading, retail firms to become multinational are many and varied. In some instances, the idiosyncratic wishes of the chairman of the company have led to such experiements. In other cases, it has been an accidental meeting at the nineteenth hole when on holiday. (There are many funny stories to be told about multinational retailing.) Other chairman have the impression that the grass is always greener elsewhere. But the firm that is to succeed in multinational retailing must, first and foremost, have a thorough mastery of a successful retail formula. This is the key element, and this probably accounts for the difference in the extent of multinational retailing in the food and the nonfood trades.

In the past decade and a half, the techniques of food retailing in Europe have been changed almost from top to bottom. The leading food retailers have had to search, adopt, and master entirely new formulas. Some fifteen years ago, the successful formula for multiple shop organizations in the food trades was a network of hundreds of small units, 40 to 50 square meters of selling space each, with a limited assortment and with a policy of saturating a given region of the country. This situation, this formula, has been completely changed, and now the new formulas of very large supermarkets and superstores or hypermarkets are being successfully mastered.

In the nonfood sector, by contrast, hardly any of the successful formulas have had to be fundamentally changed. Naturally, many improvements in the methods of operating multiple shop organizations in the footwear, men's wear, women's and children's wear trades have been made, as they have in mail order, department stores, and variety stores, but there has been no revolution in the formulas used. The mastery of existing successful formulas provided, therefore, the springboard to multinational retailing in these trades once other conditions were favorable for such developments.

What of the future? It is fairly certain that the rapidly growing mastery (and successful mastery in most cases) of the new formulas in the food trades will lead to the emergence of important multinational food retailers in Europe. In fact, if there had been no "revolution" in European food retailing in the last decades, this would already have occurred. The pioneering firms such as Gottlieb and Meinl would have been replaced by others. But the "revolution" did occur, and the leading food retailers have up to now been far too occupied with the consequences of the revolution to think seriously of other types of expansion.

The question, which firms and in what countries will the multinational operations develop, is more difficult to answer. What is clear is that individual retail firms are in danger if they stand still: they have to expand, to grow. How they grow, for example, by repetition of a successful formula and/or by diversification, and where they grow, for example, in existing markets and/or new markets, is a function of the character of the firm and of the market in which they operate.

As a generalization, it can be suggested that within the Common Market countries, the multiple shop food organizations are probably getting nearest to the limits of simple geographical expansion within national boundaries in the United Kingdom and the Netherlands. Supplementary avenues of expansion will then have to be sought. On the other hand, the multiple shop organizations in these countries have, as yet, no great experience of the newest food retailing formula, that is, the superstore or hypermarket. Combinations of the capital for expansion, on the one hand, and the know-how of formulas are therefore possible.

James B. Jefferys

APPENDIX C

Economic, Social, and Cultural Aspects of International Retailing

Let me first introduce myself as the CEO of a Dutch-based and privately held retailing company that now has a sales volume of well over $3½ billion. This clearly could not have been achieved by limiting our activities to retailing alone and to Holland with its 14 million inhabitants. Our company diversified strongly and moved into commercial banking and a wide assortment of other services that promise to grow fast—offering temporary help, cleaning offices, renting linens, catering, operating an international express service for small packages, cable television, and many, many other service outfits. Still, retailing is by far and wide the main business we are in. In this field, we branched out from our traditional department store base to food discounting and into many chains in the hard and soft goods fields. These activities are presently organized in seven divisions. We also internationalized in retailing to the United States, to Brazil, and to other countries. This is possibly why NRMA invited me to say a few words about this subject.

I feel quite honored by this invitation, which gives me a chance to philosophize twenty minutes with you about some interrelated economic, social, and cultural aspects of international retailing. I will try to keep this paper, nevertheless, as short, practical, and down to earth as possible. I will not try to be unduly optimistic. In a quickly shrinking world, retailing has been a Johnny-come-lately on the international scene: belated and not very successful. There is not much reason to believe that the outlook of internationalization of retailing will improve soon or dramatically.

The keynote of this session is stated in rather euphoric terms: World retailing is rapidly becoming an actuality as merchandising forms cross international boundaries by "exporting" their business to other countries and by acquisition of foreign firms. I doubt it. A fact is, anyhow, that retailing has been very laggard in crossing national borders, and, when it did, the results were often traumatic. Almost any human activity from the not so respectable—like the heroin trade or prostitution—to the very respectable—like hotel chains and banking—all those activities have gone

Speech delivered at the Annual Convention of National Retail Merchants Association, Tokyo, 1980. Used with permission.

international, often with spectacular success. Why not retailing? Are there specific problems to solve when one tries to internationalize retailing?

It is clear that retailing does not travel well. There is some similarity with wines. The lower qualities, the simple wines that mature quickly and don't last very long, cause few troubles when displaced. But the higher qualified and more sophisticated wines have to be transported very carefully and put to the right temperature. They should be given lots of rest and patience and love before they can regain the glory they had in their home country.

Some of the same goes for retailing forms. Some are hardy, simple, and straightforward and can be exported rather easily. Others—and mostly the interesting ones—don't travel easily. A painstaking process of translating has to be initiated; lots of patience and humility are needed to understand other markets, other internal organizations, other cultures, and to adapt oneself to them instead of the other way around. Most of the time, the success of all these efforts is only a very limited one.

The cross-pollination and dissemination of ideas in international retailing can best be illustrated by an example. I want to take you down that specific road of friendship, knowledge, and investments that has been traveled by retailing so often and in both directions: the road between the United States and Europe. In this respect, I vividly remember the retailing seminars that were given by NCR in Dayton, Ohio, back in the early 1960s. On the sound basis of scientific studies by others in the organization, the show was always stolen by a star performer, Trujillo, who extolled to whole classrooms of wide-eyed European retailers the virtues of the self-service department store. Constantly and purposely, he was poking fun at the Europeans present, who would think that dangerous developments like these could not, should not, and would not come to their continent. With a fake latino accent, he would then dramatize their disbelief and defense: "With us it is different."

Five years later the hypermarkets and Verbräuchermärkte were transforming Europe's retailing scene, ferociously and successfully attacking staid department stores, small discounters and papa and mama specialty stores at the same time. Trujillo claimed that there were no differences at all between Europe and the United States, or only a few that would not last very long. In his opinion, the basics of consumer thinking and of retailing were the same world over. That proved to be true, albeit only partly. Let us have a look at what actually has happened since World War II.

In the fifties and early sixties the road of retail information was essentially a one-way street. Europe started with a time lag in development of almost twenty years. This gap was eagerly and quickly filled, fueled by a steeply increasing standard of living. Within one generation, this standard attained the level of the United States, under the aegis of the Pax Americana and with the help of the Marshall Plan. European retailers got to know self-service and the supermarket, one-stop and one-shop shopping. Later on hard and soft goods discounting was introduced, followed by food discounting, the Levitz-type furniture store, and the home improvement center.

This dissemination was done through visits and by seminars and only sparingly by visits of American retailers to Europe and only in exceptional cases accompanied by actual participations like Jewel Tea in Belgium. The vast U.S. inland market was far more promising at that time than experiments in relatively poor countries with incomprehensible laws, quaint customs, unintelligible languages, and questionable morals, like the countries of continental Europe.

Retailers in general should be entrepreneurs who are more finely attuned and instrumented than anybody else to perceive subtle commercial and cultural differences on the international scene. Being active in the service industry, they should be the outbound, eager, adaptive, and pliable, the most studiously interested and alert entrepreneurs of them all; instead, they looked inward. Parochially. When oil, the chemical industry, the electronics industry, and many others in manufacturing went to Europe together with bankers, Madison Avenue, and even modern painters and writers, the U.S. retailers for the greater part stayed home.

Quite some information was attained by visits of Europeans to the U.S., but this was very costly at that time and was also not very efficient because most retailers soon felt lost in that gigantic American retailing maze. Information was more easily gained by attending seminars like Im Gruene in Ruschlikon near Zurich in Switzerland, where the gospel of U.S. retailing was preached for years on end. There were many zealots and proselytes in Europe, who translated all this into the European national vernacular, adapting and implementing it to their own business. The United States was the prime example, the first choice of innovation, the retailer's paradise that could be imitated freely. The United States was still way ahead: a higher standard of living, a far larger degree of mass motorization, mobility and suburbanization, less constricting zoning laws, fierce competition between older and emerging new retailing forms, less meddling by government—be it federal, state, or local—and what in the eyes of the European retailers amounted to a freedom in the later, Friedmanian, sense: freedom to choose by consumers, retailers, suppliers, everybody.

Slowly but surely the time lag diminished to one or two years. There will always be some time lag between the United States and Europe, caused by differences in market size, mobiliby, consumption patterns, buying habits, and the like. The time lag certainly has diminished in a spectacular way. Europe has dramatically increased its standard of living; it has increased in size; markets have grown even faster. The European Economic Community has virtually merged many markets into supranational ones, and it is extending its membership to other countries. Mobility has grown immensely: northern Europeans move south to the sun and their second homes; immigrant workers go northwest for jobs. Consumer aspirations have risen dramatically, being focused more and more on the international scene and gaining, in that way, in sophistication.

While climbing the mountain of wealth, the European consumer has experienced—like his American counterpart—a receding horizon behind which time and again unexpected new wants become visible, desirable, and attainable. The increase in the standard of living makes the consumer more and more aware of a disturbing fact: his growing purchasing power is being outdistanced by his list of new, unfulfilled wants, a list that has grown even longer. The wealthier he becomes, the more he feels shortchanged.

This also explains the strange phenomenon that discounting has developed in rich countries first, instead of in poor countries as one would expect. Indeed, the consumers in rich countries see so much more than those in poor countries that they more acutely experience the inadequacy of their purchasing power and then decide to do something about it. They start buying at discount for older needs, in order to save purchasing power to be spent on newly won needs. Economy is the luxury of the rich. The other side of the coin is the myopia of the consumers in most LDCs, which is pinpointed as the main cause of poverty in Galbraith's latest book: *The Nature of Mass Poverty.*

The mechanism of rising standards of living that has brought the necessity of discounting is also instrumental in what is known as the wheel of retailing. The successive expansion of new retailing forms looks somewhat like a relay race, in which muscled and fit new retailing forms take over the torch of price competition from older and tired forms. They run their round, only to arrive at the exchange point fatter and tired, where they hand over their torch again to younger runners, newer retailing forms. The increase in the standard of living and the ensuing process of trading up cause a growing need for discounting. In this way, vacuums of price competition develop at the underside of retailing markets. It is just here, where in most cases new and dynamic retailing forms slip in. They then walk into the same trap of trading up as many others did before them. This seemingly inevitable drama of evolution always ends the same. The new, aggressive form ripens, becomes established, and occupies only a limited part of the market. To use another simile, price competition in retailing is like running in quicksand: one can easily and quickly cover a few yards, but one never gets very far.

All of these mechanisms probably slow down a bit in a period of stabilizing standards of living like we are experiencing now in Europe and in the United States. Formulated in more general terms, there will be fewer retailing innovations and less international retail news in a period of stable or even waning consumer expectations. The signals are bad. The present combination of a downturn, inflation, and the energy crunch certainly will further decelerate the evolutionary processes in retailing. Most retailers will consolidate, conserve, and retrench and will try to emerge out of this bad experience with a trimmer and more efficient business.

Europe has reached a standard of living that is comparable with that of the United States, but this has been reached along a tortuous path. Along the way, its retailing firms have grown accustomed to limited resources and to political unrest, to paying ever higher wages, to the welfare state, and to the power of organized labor. In the glaring light of a critical and censorious society, retailing has learned to keep a low profile and to operate with caution.

I am not much of a futurologist. But in probing the near future, to me it seems probable that the United States and Europe will converge somewhat more than they did in the past. If such a scenario is realistic, both societies and markets will be more keenly aware of the limitations of growth, of mobility, of natural resources. Both will think smaller and will try to decentralize more. Both will want to preserve the ecology of the landscape and of townscapes, defending small, old downtowns and restricting shopping center development—a limited world indeed and a world that will be difficult to live in. But it is perhaps the most probable or the only possible one.

Europe probably will develop in the direction of the United States. Politically Europe has already veered from the Left to the middle of the road. Its citizens have lost the almost mystic neo-Keynesian belief in the insight and power of the central government. These citizens, who are better educated, more critical and individualistic than ever before, have experienced the same kind of credibility gap with their governments as U.S. citizens have with theirs. On the other hand, it is to be expected that the United States will develop somewhat in the direction of Europe. Lower growth of GNP, stronger international competition, mounting problems with inflation and energy are some of the factors behind this.

In this process of converging, U.S. retailing forms certainly will be more easily translatable in European forms, and vice-versa. It will be interesting, for instance, to see how the no-frills box store will fare and how the hypermarket will perform or the Makro type of self-service wholesaler that has been so sucessful in many other countries. This brings us back again to the general problem. Internationalization of retailing has—at least between Europe and the United States—become somewhat more like a two-way street. Even then one can wonder why so many retailing forms have successfully crossed the Atlantic, while some others—like the drug store, the automotive store, the $ store and the catalog showroom—could not.

The problems of internationalizing retailing are of quite diverse kinds. They cluster mainly around three main issues. In the first place, there are countries that are rather closely akin to each other, like the United States and Canada, and others that differ greatly in respect of their sociocultural background and in the organization of the business world, like the United States and our host country of these days. Second, retailing enterprises of some specific forms are more easily transplanted than those of other types, and the reasons for this are not always very clear. In the third place, the question is what the retailer wants to attain by internationalizing his business: a dissemination of exactly his own formula, a cheap buy in a turn-around situation, a spreading of risks?

Starting with the first set of problems, one thing is certain: retailing is about people, for people, with people. Most of the problems retailers encounter when they internationalize are qualitative in character. The cultural, sociological, and institutional differences between countries in such things as shopping habits, consumption patterns, consumer attitudes, and expectations are of prime importance. These elements are part and parcel of each local and national sociocultural structure, which is also influenced by many historical and mostly irrational forces. Retailers often don't take their time to analyze all that or at least get the vibes of the place. One needs to be sensitive in this respect, and at least to be sensible enough to focus, to adapt, to understand or—at least—to accept. These differences are sometimes large and conspicuous, and in some cases they are small and subtle. The latter ones can often be bridged only with a major effort and under greater difficulties than some of the big differences. This has not much to do with geographical distances, only with the cultural distance. It is, for instance, quite normal that a retailer from West Berlin has more problems in common with a corresponding retailer in Westwood, California, than a retailer from Amsterdam has with his colleague in Brussels. The way the business is run, the functioning of the internal organization, the inner workings of the formal and informal hierarchy, the outlook into the surrounding business world, and even the aims of the enterprise, differ from culture to culture. In this instance, they differ more between bordering Mediterranean and northern cultures in Europe than between German and American cultures half a globe apart.

Retailing is a people business in the first place. Of course, it is also a numbers business. Unfortunately, most preliminary research in international retailing is not aimed at qualitative differences at all but at numbers. What is the size of the market? Who are the main competitors and their respective market shares? What is the cost structure, and how high are maintainable margins? How is the structure of the retailing industry, and who is in command of the marketing channels? What about the costs of real estate, the construction costs, rents? Can one easily get educated, professional middle management and at what salaries? Are there laws or other barriers that limit the size of the stores or the number of outlets? And hundreds of questions more, that obscure the qualitative problems that have to be probed and solved first.

The greatest danger in international retailing is a certain ethnocentrism. Unwittingly and subconsciously, one always expects people in other countries to have the same standards in life, to behave, to act, and to react the same as the people back home. Some sensitivity and humility is needed to look and listen instead of talking and to start one's learning curve about alien peoples and cultures.

The second problem is that enterprises of some specific forms are more difficult to transplant that those in other forms. The department store and especially the fashion-oriented specialty department store is notoriously difficult in this respect. The department store is a culture mirror. When one would take away all the interior store signs, it still would be very easy to decide where a particular department store is situated geographically just by looking at the merchandising on the floor. The small differences in this respect between northern and southern Germany, between Belgium, Holland, Austria, and Great Britain, are very large and very clear to the trained eye.

Quite a few examples of transplanting department stores within Europe are known, and all of them—with no exeption—have been flops. Five different department store chains have tried to invade Holland since the beginning of this century, and all these ventures ended ignominiously in takeovers or Chapter 11. Two serious Belgian efforts in the same geographical direction since World War II were spectacularly unsuccessful. When Karstadt—Europe's largest retailer—decided to enter the French market surreptitiously and with a very low profile, it did this by teaming up with Jelmoli department stores, headquartered in Zurich, in order to enter France via their very French-speaking Geneva branch, with the intention to build jointly a department store in Lyons, only a short distance away. It is still a German store and it is losing money. There are examples galore of the difficulties that some—or, better, most—retailing businesses encounter when they are internationalized. The results of Sears in Spain are mixed at best, even while this expansion was preceded by a generation or more of experience in dealing with the Hispanic culture. J. C. Penney's own stores in Italy were not very rewarding either. The initial efforts of C&A Brenninkmeyer in the fifties, by which they cloned their successful British C&A Modes for the U.S. market, were terminated soon thereafter. After the entry of Great Britain into the Common Market, English-speaking Holland was considered to be an ideal jumping board from which to bring the blessings of advanced British retailing to a somewhat backward continent. Six, seven retailing firms crossed the channel but were back home again within a few years, wiser and poorer. Carrefour—the world's largest and most successful hypermarket chain—cannot penetrate the Federal Republic efficiently, and Dutchmen have difficulties when they want to expand into Belgium. These examples could be augmented by many more, which all illustrate the often unsurmountable difficulties encountered in the process of internationalizing retailing.

The third but also very important question is what the retailer wants to attain by internationalizing his enterprise. It can be an international cloning of his strongly profiled home formula, somewhat like Gucci or Roberta on Fifth Avenue, Marks and Spencer in Paris, Dunhill in Hong Kong or Brooks in Tokyo. If it is only a limited effort, aimed at showing the flag, selling the image abroad and doing some interesting business at the side, it should not be too difficult. In many cases it is not more than a nice ego trip. But when the retailer wants to create a business abroad of a really important size that needs an intricate organization and a large staff, it becomes different. Next to—again—C&A Brenninkmeyer in Europe, I don't know of one large-scale international cloning operation in the world that has been consistently successful.

Sometimes the international efforts is aimed at buying control of a foreign retailer, without completely transforming that enterprise. The foreign mother firm then often takes the reins of the ailing business in her own hands. Quite a few of these cases have occurred in the United States lately, and none of them have as far as yet been very successful either: Tengelmann and A&P, Mann and Fed Mart, Agache Willot and Korvettes.

Other internationalizing retailers have taken a different approach. They invest only in well-managed retailing firms, and they do this at arm's length without meddling in the day-to-day operations. In many cases they are not even too keen to get the majority or even control of the company. They are only interested in keeping the management motivated and maintaining a good investment. This promises old-fashioned synergies between the two firms by starting learning processes for both parties. The essentially low-profit approach has been the policy of our company in international matters.

Often there is an element of spreading uncertainties internationally. One should distinguish here between risk and uncertainty. Risks can be evaluated and therefore one can insure oneself against risks. Risks should be avoided, but this is not the case with uncertainties. The magnitude of uncertainties cannot be rationally evaluated. Uncertainties should not be avoided; they should be spread, not in order to avoid them but to make better use of them. Uncertainties are a main cause and justification of profits. Accepting uncertainties is essential to private enterprise. Uncertainty is not a risk and not an alibi, it is a chance and chances are here for the taking.

It is essentially this chancy venturing out into new territories, that is the charm and seduction of international retailing. It is exacting for higher management because what is needed is a cool head and at the same time a capacity to dream. One has to act quickly, but not in a hurry, and one has to have some modesty to start one's own learning processes anew at a riper age. International retailing is as difficult as it is fascinating and I, personally, am gald that I am in this kind of business.

A.C.R. Dreesmann

Bibliography

"A & P Looks Like Tengelmann's Vietnam." *Business Week*, February 1, 1982, p. 42.

"A & P's Busy Boss." *Business Week*, August 3, 1981, p. 32.

"A & P: Should You Invest Along with the Germans?" *Financial World*, February 1, 1979, pp. 16-20.

"Austin Reed Gears Toward the 20 Year Old Male." *Marketing*, November 24, 1983, p. 18.

Barmash, Isadore. *More Than They Bargained For: The Rise and Fall of Korvettes.* New York: Lebhar-Friedman Books, 1981.

_____. "The Invasion of the Corporate Body Snatchers." *New York Times*, February 25, 1979.

Bata, Thomas J. "Retailing Around the World—The Opportunities, the Challenges." Address to the World Conference of Retailing, Toronto, April 19, 1982.

"B.A.T. Says Net Rose 18% in 1982: Revenue Up 24%." *Wall Street Journal*, April 8, 1983; p. 32.

Batus. *Annual Report 1981.*

"Batus Changes Wipe Out Field's Retailing Identity." *Advertising Age*, August 2, 1982, pp. 36-37E.

"Batus Retail Operating Net Carves Out 31% Gain; Sales Up." *Women's Wear Daily*, April 20, 1984, p. 2.

Berenbeium, Ronald. "Managing the International Company: Building a Global Perspective." *The Conference Board*, New York, 1982.

"Big Warehouse Outlet Breaks Traditional Rules of Retailing." *Wall Street Journal*, December 22, 1983, p. 27.

"A Bit of Tengel." *Economist*, April 19, 1980, p. 66.

Boddewyn, J. J. "Global Spread of Advertising Regulation." *MSU Business Topics* (Spring 1981): 5-13.

Boddewyn, J. J., and Stanley C. Hollander, eds. *Public Policy toward Retailing.* Lexington, Mass.: Lexington Books, D. C. Heath and Company, 1972.

"British Food Marketing—The Winning Ways of Brand X." *Economist*, September 4, 1982, p. 72.

"British Supermarkets Turn to Non-Foods More and More." *Chain Store Age Executive* (May 1980): 115.

"Brothers Who Want Korvettes." *New York Times*, February 4, 1979, sec. 3, pp. 1-7.

"Burger King Preparing to Open 300 New Units in Europe by 1987." *Restaurant News,* November 21, 1983, p. 18.

"Business Briefs." *Wall Street Journal*, April 29, 1981, p. 48.

Cateora, Philip R. *International Marketing*. New York: Richard D. Irwin, 1983.

"The Changing Face of Marketing." *Marketing*, December 1, 1983, p. 30.

Cherkasky, William B. "Franchising Goes International." *Business America*, November 1, 1982, p. 34.

Clark, Eric. "Conran's Dual Challenge." *Marketing*, August 5, 1982, p. 19.

"Common Market Nations Decide to Drop Trade Sanctions against Soviet Union." *Wall Street Journal*, December 23, 1983, p. 12.

"A Countdown Starts for Gimbels." *Business Week*, April 2, 1979, p. 78.

Crovitz, Gordon. "Europe Pays for Its Pipe Dream." *Wall Street Journal*, December 13, 1983, p. 30.

Davidson, William R., Albert D. Bates, and Stephen J. Bass. "The Retail Life Cycle." *Harvard Business Review* (November-December, 1976): 93.

Davies, Ross L., ed. *Retail Planning in the European Community*. Farnborough, England: Saxon House, 1979.

Dawson, John A. "Public Policy Controls Hypermarket Development." Paper presented to the World Marketing Congress, Nova Scotia, Canada, November 3-5, 1983.

————. "Structural-Spatial Relationships in the Spread of Hypermarket Retailing." In E. Kaynak and R. Savitt, eds., *Comparative Marketing Systems*. New York: Praeger, 1984.

Delhaize Freres & Cie "Le Lion" S.A. *Annual Report 1981*. Brussels, 1982.

Dietrich, Robert. "The Rethinking of the Supermarket," *Progressive Grocer,* December 1982, pp. 49-67.

"Discounters Buy Rather Than Build." *Chain Store Age Executive* (July 1982): 28.

"European Community—The Impurities Are Not Just in the Beer." *Economist*, October 22, 1983, p. 49.

"European Industrial Policy: Past, Present and Future." *Conference Board in Europe* (February 1980): 51.

"European Industry and Multinationals: New Spirit of Cooperation." *Multinational Info.*, Institute for Research and Information on Multinationals, Paris, no. 2, (May 1983): 6.

"European Target Specialty Chains." *Chain Store Age Executive* (January 1982): 68-69.

"Europe in the 1980s—Corporate Forecasts and Strategies." *Business International S.A.* (February 1979): 13-20, 103, 105.

"Europe Moves to Harmonize Communication." *Wall Street Journal*, January 23, 1984, p. 27.

"Europe Still Eyes the U.S." *Supermarket News*, June 14, 1982, p. 10.

"Feedstuffs." *Minneapolis*, October 19, 1981, p. 8.

Frank, Isaiah. *Foreign Enterprises in Developing Countries*. Baltimore: Johns Hopkins University Press, 1953.

"The Fraying End of Woolies' Yarn." *Economist*, September 25, 1982, pp. 80-85.

Fry, Earl H. *Financial Invasion of the U.S.A.* New York: McGraw-Hill, 1980.

Fuller, C. W. F. Baden. *Rising Concentration: Are Fears Justified?* U.K. Grocery Trade 1970-80, Research in Marketing Series. London: London Business School, July 1982.

"A German Expands in U.S. Retailing." *Business Week*, August 15, 1977, p. 34.

"German Mail Order Firms Eye U.S." *Wall Street Journal*, March 2, 1982, p. 35.

"Gloom for Shopping Complexes." *Marketing*, December 16, 1982, p. 8.

"Golden Touches to Lead." *Time*, November 30, 1981, p. 66.

Guy, C. M. *Retail Location and Retail Planning in Britain.* Farnborough, England: Gower Publishing Company, 1980.

Hackett, Donald W. "The International Expansion of U.S. Franchise Systems: Status and Strategies." *Journal of International Business Studies* (Spring 1976): 65-75.

Harrison, Gilbert W. "Retail Mergers." *Mergers and Acquisition* (Winter 1983): 40-50.

Hollander, Stanley C. *Multinational Retailing.* MSU International Business and Economic Studies. East Lansing: Michigan State University, 1970.

Hone, Angus, and Andreas Schlapfer. *Marketing in Europe.* Geneva: International Trade Center. UNTCAD/GATT, 1974.

Hower, Ralph M. *History of Macy's of New York, 1858-1919.* Cambridge, Mass.: Harvard University Press, 1943.

"International Association of Department Stores." *Retail News Letter* (Paris) (July 1981): 8; (November 1981): 12.

Kacker, Madhav. "Benefits Uncertain in European Acquisition of U.S. Retailers." *Marketing News*, March 4, 1983, p. 8.

_____. *Marketing and Economic Development.* New Delhi: Deep & Deep Publications, 1982.

_____. *Transatlantic Investment in Retailing*, The Conference Board, Research Bulletin no. 138, New York, 1983.

"*KBB in Outline.*" Amsterdam, 1981.

"KFC Wooing the Swiss Family." *Advertising Age*, January 25, 1982, p. 64.

"K mart Gets 44% of Mexican Chain." *Playthings*, September 1981, p. 12.

Lifflander, Mathew L. *It's Getting Popular, Franchising Around the World*, vol. 4 (September 1970), p. 15.

Lil' Champ. *Annual Report, 1982.*

"McDonald's: The Original Recipe Helps It Defy a Downturn." *Business Week*, May 4, 1981, pp. 161-164.

"A Magnet Moves His Empire across the Sea." *Business Week*, May 31, 1982, p. 39.

Mahoney, Tom, and Leonard Sloane. *The Great Merchants.* New York: Harper & Row, 1974.

"Merger of 2 Gimbels by Batus." *Women's Wear Daily*, March 22, 1983, pp. 1, 10.

Michel, David. "Development in the Structure of Distribution in France, a Modest Degree of Concentration." *Journal of Retailing* (Summer 1965): 34-44.

Le Movement du Commerce Associé, AFRESCO: Chaines Voluntaires, *Societies Cooperatives de Detaillants*, AFRESCO study 213, Paris 1973.

National Planning Association. *U.S. Business Performance Abroad—The Case Study of Sears Roebuck Company*, Washington, D.C.: The Association, 1953.

"News Brief." *Wall Street Journal*, April 29, 1982, p. 48.

New York Times, February 25, 1979.

Nichols, John P. *Skyline Queen and the Merchant Prince: The Woolworth Story.* New York: Trident Press, 1973.

Pepsi Company Inc. *Annual Report, 1982.*

"The Progress of Scanning." *Retailing Today* (July 1982): 2.

Promodes. *Rapport Annual, 1981.*

"A Revived Miller-Wohl Lures a Dutch Bidder." *Business Week,* September 5, 1977, p. 34.

Safeway. *Annual Report, 1981.*

"Saks Expansion Set: Cost $200 Million." *New York Times*, February 23, 1979, p. D1.

Sears, Roebuck & Co. *Annual Report, 1981.*

———. *The Sears International Story.* Chicago: Sears, Roebuck and Co., 1980.

"Sears to Increase Holding to 60.5% in Simpson Sears." *Wall Street Journal,* June 10, 1983, p. 4.

Servan-Schreiber, Jean Jacques. *The American Challenge,* New York: Atheneum, 1968.

Sheth, Jagdish N. "Emerging Trends for the Retailing Industry." *Journal of Retailing* (Fall 1983): 14.

"Star-Spangled Menace." *Marketing Magazine*, February 1, 1969.

"A Supermarket without a Store." *Business Week*, January 11, 1964, pp. 100-102.

Terpstra, Vern. *The Cultural Environment of International Business.* Cincinnati: South Western Publishing, 1978.

Thurow, Roger. "German Firms Cultivate Soviet Trade." *Wall Street Journal,* November 16, 1983, p. 34.

Trotta, A. Leonides, ed., *Retailing International, 1969-1970.* New York: National Retail Merchants Association, 1969.

U.S. Department of Commerce. "Selected Data on the Operations of U.S. Affiliates of Foreign Companies." *1978 and 1979 Survey of Current Business* (July 1980): 36; (May 1981): 35-52.

———. International Trade Administration. *Attracting Foreign Investment to the United States.* Washington, D.C.: Government Printing Office, 1981.

———. *Foreign Direct Investment in the United States.* Report to the Congress. Washington, D.C.: Government Printing Office, April 1976.

———. *Foreign Direct Investment in the United States, 1980 and 1981 Transactions.* Washington, D.C.: Government Printing Office, October 1981, December 1982.

———. *Franchising in the Economy, 1980-82.* Washington, D.C.: Government Printing Office, January 1982.

———. Office of International Investment. *OPEC Direct Investment in the United States.* Washington, D.C.: Government Printing Office, November 1981.

Vaughn, Charles L. *Franchising.* Lexington, Mass.: Lexington Books, D.C. Heath and Company, 1979.

Videotex. "What It's All About." *Marketing News.* November 25, 1983, p. 16.

Vroom & Dreesmann. *Annual Report, 1980-81, 1981-82.*

"Vroom, Vroom." *Economist*, January 12, 1980, p. 74.

Waldman, Charles. *Strategies of International Mass Retailers.* New York: Praeger Publishers, 1978.

Walker, Bruce J., and Michael J. Etzel. "The Internationalization of U.S. Franchise Systems: Progress and Procedures." *Journal of Marketing* (April 1973): 38-46.

Wall Street Journal. December 1, 1982, p. 40.

_____. April 8, 1983, p. 32.

Wax, Allan J. "White Knights Grow Scarce." *Newsday*, April 17, 1983, p. 84.

Weil, Gordon L. *Sears, Roebuck, U.S.A.* New York: Stein & Day, 1977.

"West German Retailing—Upmarket on Downhill." *Economist*, July 2, 1983, p. 64.

What Will Tomorrow's Customers Want? Mann GmbH, Karlsruhe 1, West Germany, 1978, p. 21.

"Who's Buying What?" *Chain Store Executive* (August 1981): 10.

Winje, Dietmar K. "European Still High on Soviet Gas." *Wall Street Journal*, December 28, 1983, p. 13.

Winkler, John K. "*Five and Ten: The Fabulous Life of F. W. Woolworth.* New York: Robert M. McBridge & Company, 1940.

Wood, Peter W., and Robert F. Elliot. "Trading Blocs and Common Markets." In Ingo Walter and Tracy Murray, eds. *Handbook of International Business*, pp. 4-42. New York: John Wiley, 1982.

F. W. Woolworth Company. *Annual Report, 1979.*

_____. *Annual Report, 1981.*

_____. *Fifty Years of Woolworth (1879-1929).* New York: F. W. Woolworth, 1929.

"Woolworth Holdings on Its Marks." *Economist*, September 17, 1983, p. 77.

Index

ABOUT THE AUTHOR

MADHAV P. KACKER, currently on the faculty of Suffolk University's School of Management in Boston, has also taught in India as well as at other American universities. He was a visiting professor at Hofstra University and Michigan Technological University, and a Fulbright Fellow at Baruch College, City University of New York. He has published *Marketing and Economic Development, Marketing Adaptation of U.S. Business Firms in India, Marketing of Cotton Piecegoods in India,* and articles on international marketing.

TRANSATLANTIC TRENDS IN RETAILING

Takeovers and Flow of Know-How

MADHAV P. KACKER

Since 1975, over one billion dollars' worth of foreign money has poured into the American retailing industry, the bulk of it from Western European countries. Much of it was in the form of a direct takeover. American retailing giants such as Grand Union, Gimbels, Saks Fifth Avenue, A & P Stores, Fed Mart, Korvettes, and others were acquired by foreign companies. These acquisitions were reported in the American press, not simply as financial news, but as major stories focusing on the "weakness" of the American firms and the "clout" being wielded by foreign investors. It was assumed that this tremendous influx of foreign dollars would be met by fear and dismay by the general public and anger on the part of many U.S. industries. Interestingly, Kacker found that many U.S. retailers welcomed the foreign capital. Kacker stressed the synergy derived from new concepts of organization and management and the challenge to grow which foreign acquisition provided, while cautioning entrepreneurs about the culturally-specific traditions and national regulations which effected successful retailing. Most participants in the game were not newcomers to internationalization, take-overs, or retailing. And while the trend has slowed somewhat, foreign investment, acquisition, and input into the American retailing industry continues.

Transatlantic Trends in Retailing offers the complete picture—past, present, and future—of this